Every Pilgrim's Guide to Oberammergau

and its Passion Play

MICHAEL COUNSELL

illustrated by
CHAN BOREY

CANTERBURY PRESS
PRESS
Norwich

Text © Michael Counsell 1998
Illustrations © Chan Borey 1998
Maps © John Flower 1998

Photographs of the 1990 Passion Play © Thomas Klinger 1998,
used by kind permission of the Village Committee.
Other photographs © Michael Counsell 1998

First published 1998 by The Canterbury Press Norwich
(a publishing imprint of Hymns Ancient & Modern Limited,
a registered charity)
St Mary's Works, St Mary's Plain,
Norwich, Norfolk, NR3 3BH

British Library Cataloguing in Publication Data

A catalogue record for this book is available
from the British Library

ISBN 1–85311–213–5

*Photoset by Rowland Phototypesetting Limited
Bury St Edmunds, Suffolk
Printed and bound in Great Britain by
Biddles Limited, Guildford and King's Lynn*

Contents

Preface

To re-enact the last week of the life of Jesus of Nazareth is a widespread tradition. Passion plays have been particularly common in the foothills of the Alps, in the high mountain valleys of Bavaria, in southern Germany, and in the northern province of Austria called the Tyrol.

This book concentrates on the world-famous Passion Play which is performed every ten years in the Bavarian village of Oberammergau. The book was written and photographed for the most part during the season of the 1990 Oberammergau production. It will serve, therefore, to remind those who saw that production of their moving experience. They can also show it to their friends and so share with them what it meant to be in the Passion Play Theatre.

The book may also be a small compensation to those who were unable to obtain tickets for Oberammergau in 1990. Those who were sure of a seat were those who booked early, through a tour operator who paid the Village authorities for tickets two years in advance.

This book may also whet the appetite of those who would like to see the production in the year AD 2000 and may encourage them to make plans in good time. About half a million people will see the Oberammergau Passion Play at about a hundred performances, five times a week, between 22 May and 1 October 2000.

The millennium year will be celebrated in many different ways. Although the arithmetic may not be quite accurate, it is supposed to mark the two thousandth anniversary of the birth of Jesus. What better way could there be to celebrate our entry into the third millennium than to watch a reverent representation of the death and resurrection of Jesus – which he himself said was the purpose of his birth and the meaning of history?

At the end of the book there is a list of other places which have regular passion plays. Because they are not so well known they are not as crowded as the one at Oberammergau. A holiday in Bavaria or the Tyrol is enjoyable at any time, but combined with a visit to a Passion play, it can become a spiritual experience.

Michael Counsell
Honor Oak, London, 1998

Author's Notes

In this book 'the Village' with a capital 'V' always means the village of Oberammergau in Bavaria; 'the Play' means the Passion Play enacted there every ten years; and 'the Theatre' means the Passionspielhaus where it is performed.

Each section opens with a brief summary and usually ends with a prayer for personal or group use.

All Bible passages marked with '(NRSV)' have been quoted from the New Revised Standard Version. Other Bible passages have been retranslated by the author.

A selection of hymns is included at the end of the book. These may be used in churches in Oberammergau or during the journeys to and from the Village.

The general information supplied – in particular the arrangements in the Village, opening and closing times and telephone numbers – was carefully checked at the time of writing, but inevitably some details may vary from time to time.

The two indexes at the end of the book should enable the reader to find with ease the information required.

Acknowledgements

The author thanks the following individuals and organizations for their help in the preparation of this book:

- the German Tourist Office in London;
- the Oberammergau Village Committee;
- Inter-Church Travel Ltd, who sponsored the Ecumenical Centre in 1990;
- the artists who prepared the maps and drawings;
- the people of the Village;
- and all the volunteer ministers who went to staff the Centre, from whom I learned so much about the love of God.

Useful Information

TICKETS

The Oberammergau Passion Play is performed every ten years.
Tickets for the Play can only be obtained through tour operators
who have bought them two years in advance. Turning up at
the Village and hoping to buy tickets there usually leads to
frustration. Nevertheless, it is a delightful place to visit in
non-Play years.

GENERAL INFORMATION FOR VISITORS TO GERMANY

German National Tourist Office

General information about visiting Germany can be obtained from
the German National Tourist Office, 65 Curzon Street, London
W1Y 8NE. Open 12 noon to 5 p.m. Tel: 0891 600100 for brochure
requests without delay; premium (higher) charges apply to calls on
this number. Live operator service from 10 a.m. to 12 noon and
2 p.m. to 4 p.m. Tel: 0171 493 0080. Fax: 0171 495 6129.
E-mail: German_National_Tourist_Office@compuserve.com
Internet: http://www.germany-tourism.de

Tourist Board of Bavaria

Information about visiting Bavaria can be obtained from the
Tourist Board of Bavaria, D-80535 München, Germany.
Tel: 08921 23 9730. Fax: 08929 3582. See also the section on
Munich below (p. 24).
E-mail: tourismus@bayern.btl.de
Internet: http://www.btl.de/bayern

Most German towns have a Tourist Information Centre indicated
by the international 'i' symbol.

The following sections are listed in alphabetical order:

Church opening hours

Most churches in Bavaria open from Monday to Saturday, 9 a.m.
to 5.30 p.m. They are only open on Sundays during services, when
you are welcome to worship, but it is discourteous to wander
around.

Conversion table

From	To	Multiply by	
Inches	Centimetres	2.54	0.3937
Feet	Metres	0.3048	3.2808
Yards	Metres	0.9144	1.0936
Miles	Kilometres	1.6090	0.6214
Acres	Hectares	0.4057	2.4649
Gallons	Litres	4.5460	0.2200
Ounces	Grams	28.35	0.0353
Pounds	Grams	453.6	0.0022
Pounds	Kilograms	0.4536	2.2046
Tons	Tonnes	1.0160	0.9843
To	From		Multiply by

Distances are measured in kilometres (km.); approximately
8 km. = 5 miles; 1 km. = 0.62 miles; 100 km. = 62.14 miles.

Electrical equipment

Current is 220 volts AC. Plug sockets are of the European two-
pronged design, so a travel adaptor is necessary. Airlines require
electrical equipment to be carried in hand luggage. See also 'Radio
reception' below. Films and batteries can be bought everywhere.

Emergencies

(See below under 'Telephoning' for telephoning to Germany from
the UK.)

British Embassy, Friedrich-Ebert-Allee 77, D-53113 Bonn,
Germany. Tel: (49) (228) 9167-0. Fax: 9167-200. Office hours
(GMT): 0700–1100 and 1200–1530.

British Consulate-General, Burkleinstraße 10, D-80538 München,
Germany. Tel: (49) (89) 211090. Fax: 21109 166. Office hours
(GMT): winter 0730–1100 and 1200–1600; summer 0630–1000
and 1100–1500.

Details of all British Representatives abroad and travel advice can
be found on the Internet at http://www.fco.gov.uk

Note: The double-'s' sound in German is often written as *ß*, so that
Straße is pronounced 'Shtraasseh'. (Not after a short 'a' in *Gasse* or
Sparkasse, but the rules are changing.) The house number follows
the street name.

Emergency telephone numbers in Germany
Police: 110
Fire Brigade, Emergency Ambulance and Medical Emergencies: 112
But in less urgent situations call the local ambulance service, using the local telephone number where it is listed under towns referred to in this book or the telephone directory.

Finance

German banking hours are generally Monday to Friday, 8.30 a.m. to 4 p.m., closing for lunch from 1 p.m. to 2.30 p.m. But in Bavaria it is more often 8.30 a.m. to 12.30 p.m. and 1.30 p.m. to 3.30 p.m., and on Thursdays they stay open until 5.30 p.m. They are closed on Saturdays and Sundays.

There are 100 pfennigs (pf.) to 1 Deutschmark (DM). By 2000 they will be in the process of changing to the Euro, which they pronounce 'Oy-roe'.

You can change traveller's cheques in exchange bureaux (marked *Wechsel*), some (but not all) banks, major post offices and some hotels, but not in guest-houses. Always keep a note of the numbers of your traveller's cheques in a separate place.

You can also draw cash with Visa cards or MasterCards through machines outside certain banks. It is advisable to buy a small amount of German marks before setting out. There is no limit on the amount in notes that you can change back into sterling when you return.

Health

Vaccinations and inoculations are not normally necessary, but visitors should take with them any medicines or other health-related items which they may require.

Travellers should obtain a copy of the booklet T5, *Health advice for travellers*, available from major Post Offices in the UK. They should follow its advice, complete the Form E111 which is included in it, have it stamped and signed by the Post Office, and keep it with their passport.

To obtain free health care in Germany see page 41 of booklet T5. It may be necessary to contact a local German insurance company first, and your Tour Operator or the local information office should advise you on that. See the T5 booklet for other countries also.

Doctors' surgery hours in Germany are generally from 10 a.m. to 12 noon and 4 p.m. to 6 p.m., except for Wednesdays and the weekend. For urgent cases call the emergency service, using the local telephone number obtained from the local information office or the telephone directory. If there is no time to see a doctor first, a patient's E111 should be shown to the hospital on admission.

Dispensing chemist shops or pharmacies (*Apotheke*) have a flashing green cross outside and a night-opening rota displayed in the window.

The mains water is drinkable, but if you have a delicate stomach you are advised to buy bottled water.

Language

More German people speak English than English people speak German. See 'Learn a Phrase a Day' below (p. 111).

Poste restante

Letters or packages marked *Postlagernd* will be kept at the main post office of the town for up to four weeks.

Radio reception

The BBC World Service can be received on 3955 kHz, 6195 kHz, 7325 kHz, 9410 kHz*, 9915 kHz, and 12095 kHz* on short wave and 648 kHz medium wave in Western Europe (* denotes the longest broadcast time). Further details from the BBC World Service Shop, Bush House, Strand, PO Box 76, London WC2B 4PH. Tel: 0171 257 2576. Fax: 0171 240 4811.
e-mail: worldservice.shop@bbc.co.uk
Internet: http://www.bbc.co.uk/worldservice

Bayerischer Rundfunk frequencies in Oberammergau are: (Classical) 93.10 kHz; (Modern Music) 96.10 kHz: (Easy Listening) 87.7 kHz.

Security

Although crime is no worse in Germany than elsewhere, you are advised to keep handbags, cameras, travel documents and passports attached to your person so as not to leave them behind anywhere.

Shops

Shops in Germany are usually open Mondays to Fridays from 9 a.m. to 6.30 p.m. and on Thursdays until 8 p.m., but some shops close from about 12 noon to 2 p.m. On Saturdays smaller shops open from about 9 a.m. to 2 p.m., and larger stores from 9 a.m. to 4 p.m.

Sizes

Below are the approximately corresponding sizes in different countries.

Ladies' outer clothing

Germany & Holland	UK	France & Belgium	Spain	Italy & Scand.	Japan	USA
34	8/30	38	40	36	7	6
36	10/32	40	42	38	9	8
38	12/34	42	44	40	11	10
40	14/36	44	46	42	13	12
42	16/38	46	48	44	15	14
44	18/40	48	50	46	17	16

Shoes

Europe	UK	Japan	USA women	USA men
36	3	22	4 ½	
37	4	23	5 ½	
38	5	24	6 ½	
39	6	25	7 ½	6 ½
40	7		8 ½	7 ½
41	8			8 ½
42	9			9 ½
43	10			10 ½

Men's outer clothing and shirts

Outer clothing		**Shirts**	
Europe	UK/USA	Europe	UK/USA
46	36	36	14
48	38	37	14 ½
50	40	38	15
52	42	39	15 ½
54	44	40	16
56	46	41	16 ½
		42	17
		43	17 ½

Telephones

You can make local and long-distance phone calls from post offices and public call-boxes. Most kiosks accept phone cards, which you can purchase at any post office for 12 or 50 DM.

To telephone to the United Kingdom from Germany: dial 0044, then the full UK number without the first 0. If you have a telephone chargecard from BT or one of the other UK telephone companies, they will tell you a number to dial direct from Germany to connect to an English-speaking operator, but it is better to do this from a public telephone rather than from an hotel. Certain networks of British mobile telephones work in Germany, but not all. (Don't take a mobile phone into the Theatre!)

When telephoning to Germany from the UK, dial 0049, then omit the first 0. For Bonn telephone 0228 from Germany, 0049228 from the UK. For Munich telephone 089 from Germany, 004989 from the UK. For Oberammergau telephone 08822 from Germany, 00498822 from the UK.

Temperatures

Temperatures in Germany are measured in degrees Celsius or Centigrade: $0°C = 32°F$; $10°C = 50°F$; $20°C = 68°F$; $50°C = 122°F$; $100°C = 212°F$.

Time

European time is one hour in advance of Britain.

Tipping and etiquette

A recent German Tourist Board publication contains the following advice: 'Tipping in Germany is purely voluntary (up to 10% of the total bill). It means you are expressing your particular satisfaction with the service you've received. All you need to know on the subject of etiquette is to maintain an attitude of polite reserve, to use the polite "Sie" form of address if you speak German and to shake hands when you greet someone.'

INFORMATION FOR VISITORS TO OBERAMMERGAU

Oberammergau Tourist Information Office (associated with the abr-travel agency), Ammergauer Haus, Eugen-Papst-Straße 9a, D-82487 Oberammergau, Germany. Open Monday to Friday 8.30 a.m. to 6 p.m., Saturday 8.30 a.m. to 12 noon. Tel: 9231-0. Fax: 7325. The office can give information on accommodation in non-Play years and addresses of doctors, dentists etc.

Information on Oberammergau (much of it in English) is also available on the Internet at this website: http://www.oberammergau.de

---

Emergency telephone numbers in Oberammergau
(Dial 08822 from outside the Village.)
Police: Feldiglgasse 17. Tel: 6081 (in emergencies 110)
Fire: 112
Ambulance: 19222
Mountain rescue: 6333

The following sections are listed in alphabetical order:

Accommodation

In Play years, accommodation in the region is almost unobtainable without advance booking. At other times contact the *Verkehrsbüro* (travel office) in each town for details of hotels and guest houses.

Banks in Oberammergau

Hypo-Bank, Dorfstraße 3. Tel: 92900. Kreissparkasse, Dorfstraße 23. Tel: 92040. Raiffeisenbank, Bahnhofstraße 24. Tel: 92110. All three banks have cash machines.

See 'Finance' above for banking hours. Don't rely on reaching the front of the queue at the bank before it closes for lunch.

Bicycle hire

Oberammergau Sports Centre. Tel: 4178. Ammergauer Radlladen. Tel: 1428.

Cabin cable car

From the WellenBerg swimming pool up the Laber (1,684 metres) to the mountain restaurant. 9–11.50 a.m. and 1–4.30 p.m. (1–5 p.m. in June, 1–5.30 p.m. in July and August). Tel: 4770.

Chair-lift

To the Kolbensattel (1,270 metres). 9–11.45 a.m. and 1–4.45 p.m. in the summer; 9 a.m. – 4.30 p.m. in the ski season. Tel: 4760. Mountain hut and snack bar at the summit.

Chemist shops

Kofel-Apotheke, Ettalerstraße 12. Tel: 6664. Sternapotheke, Dorfstraße 5. Tel: 3540 or 4190.

Climate

Bavaria lies at a high altitude, and so temperatures can be colder than those in Britain. Visitors to the Play will be sitting for long periods of time in the open air, so layers of warm clothing which can be added or removed are recommended, as are a waterproof coat and comfortable waterproof footwear. But be prepared also for swimming and sunbathing at the pool in Oberammergau, or elsewhere on your journey.

Craft Museum

The Heimatsmuseum, Dorfstraße 8. Open in the summer 2–6 p.m., closed on Mondays; open in the winter 2–6 p.m. on Saturdays only. Tel: 94136. In non-Play years you can buy a single ticket to include both the Craft Museum and a tour of the Theatre.

Getting there

Visitors in Play years can only spend one or at most two nights in or near Oberammergau, so most tours include a holiday in southern Germany or the neighbouring countries. Most visitors will come to the Village by coach and will be taken to their pre-booked accommodation in Oberammergau or the surrounding villages, and will be brought to the Theatre by coach also. It is also possible to approach by car from Munich (München) along the A95 (E533) autobahn and then on highway B2 towards Garmisch-Partenkirchen, but turning off at Oberau onto the B23 to Oberammergau. Alternatively, travel by train from Munich, see under 'Railway Station' below.

Lost property

Go to Schnitzlergasse 6, opposite the Town Hall.

The Passion Play Theatre

Tel: 32278 for opening hours and guided tours in non-Play years.

The Pilatushaus

See woodcarvers and other craftsmen at work. Open Monday to Friday, 1–6 p.m. in the summer. Admission free. Tel: 1682 for details.

Post office

Deutsche Bundespost, Rottenbucherstraße 36. Tel: 3061. Open 8 a.m. to 6 p.m. Monday to Friday and 8 a.m. to 12 noon on Saturday.

Useful Information

Railway station

Tel: 3513. Trains are hourly to and from Munich changing at Murnau, and the journey takes 48 minutes.

Souvenirs

Oberammergau is famous for its wood-carvings, and you can buy some delightful toys, Christmas cribs and decorations, and clocks. But they are not cheap, so allow enough currency or credit cards to bring back what you want. Also available are embroidery, *dirndl* dresses, Tyrolean hats and other outdoor clothing, and, of course, books, postcards, transparencies and cassettes of the Passion Play. There are videos about the local region but not about the Play. UK visitors should be sure to buy the British PAL version of videos.

Taxis

Richter, Welfengasse 2. Tel: 94294.
Götz, Knableiten 10. Tel: 94440.

The WellenBerg Leisure Centre

Swimming pools, sauna, solarium, hot-air balloon etc. Open daily 9.30 a.m. to 8 p.m. Tel: 6787.

Location of Oberammergau in Europe

Mystery Plays

The Oberammergau Passion Play is an example of the mystery plays of the Middle Ages. Few people today are familiar with this form of drama, but to appreciate fully what happens in Oberammergau one needs to know something about the background.

Liturgical drama

Although the Christian Church resisted the classical theatre of Greece and Rome because of its association with immorality, the origins of modern drama are to be found in Church liturgy. The Holy Communion, Eucharist or Mass is a regular re-enactment or re-presentation, as Jesus commanded us, of the Last Supper which he had with his disciples. At Easter, in particular, the priests of medieval times made a symbolic visit to a part of the church building representing the tomb where Jesus was buried. There they would act out the women disciples' early morning search for the body of the Christ.

'The poor man's Bible'

In a period when few people could read the Scriptures, liturgical drama, along with stone carving and stained-glass windows, became the 'poor man's Bible'. In many places the dramas grew into spectacles lasting all day, portraying the whole life of Christ, and performed on carts and temporary stages at various places around the town. Each scene was allocated to an appropriate trade guild. For instance, the schoolmasters might re-enact the incident in which the twelve-year-old Jesus disputed with the teachers of the law in the Temple, and the carpenters might be responsible for the crucifixion scene.

'Mystery'

These were called 'mystery plays', a name derived from St Paul's use of the word 'mystery' to mean God's secret plan to save people from sin and death by the life and death of Jesus, now revealed and made public to everyone. The texts of the medieval cycles of plays are preserved in York, Coventry and some other places in England, where in recent years they have been regularly performed. The well-known *Coventry Carol* comes from the Coventry Mystery Plays, and is the lullaby sung by the mothers of Bethlehem to their babies who were about to be slaughtered by King Herod's soldiers. There is a similar re-enactment of the life of Christ in the Ascension Day procession at Bruges in Belgium, where the different scenes follow one another around the streets before the spectators.

Passion plays

Instead of representing the whole of Christ's life, the Alpine region concentrated on the events of his last week. These Alpine plays are called 'passion plays', from the Latin word *passus* meaning 'suffered'. We use the word in the same way in the name of the passion flower, parts of which resemble the nails, whips and crown of thorns from the story of the crucifixion of Jesus.

The people of the middle ages wanted a good number of demons in their passion plays so they usually concluded with a scene of the Last Judgement. These scenes seem crude to modern tastes, so they have usually been excised from the texts which are performed today.

Oberammergau

Oberammergau nestles in the valley of the River Ammer in the Bavarian mountains. The Village is dominated by the Parish Church and the Theatre where the famous Passion Plays are performed. Unlike those in many other communities today, the people in places like this, where religious drama is regularly performed, all know the facts on which their faith is based.

The stage at the passion play.

Matthew 26:20–29

On the first day of Unleavened Bread the disciples came to Jesus, saying, 'Where do you want us to make the preparations for you to eat the Passover?' He said, 'Go into the city to a certain man, and say to him, "The Teacher says, My time is near; I will keep the Passover at your house with my disciples."' So the disciples did as Jesus had directed them, and they prepared the Passover meal. When it was evening, he took his place with the twelve; and while they were eating, he said, 'Truly I tell you, one of you will betray me.' And they became greatly distressed and began to say to him one after another, 'Surely not I, Lord?' He answered, 'The one who has dipped his hand into the bowl with me will betray me. The Son of Man goes as it is written of him, but woe to that one by whom the Son of Man is betrayed! It would have been better for that one not to have been born.' Judas, who betrayed him, said, 'Surely not I, Rabbi?' He replied, 'You have said so.'

While they were eating, Jesus took a loaf of bread, and after blessing it he broke it, gave it to the disciples, and said, 'Take, eat; this is my body.' Then he took a cup, and after giving thanks he gave it to them, saying, 'Drink from it, all of you; for this is my blood of the covenant, which is poured out for many for the forgiveness of sins. I tell you, I will never again drink of this fruit of the vine until that day when I drink it new with you in my Father's kingdom.' (NRSV)

Prayer

Assist us mercifully with your help, O Lord God of our salvation, that we may enter with joy upon the contemplation of those mighty acts, whereby you have given us life and immortality; through Jesus Christ our Lord. Amen.

From the *Gelasian Sacramentary*

3

The Plague

The Oberammergau Passion Play is unique because it has been performed regularly without interruption for over 350 years, and because it originated with a vow made to God in 1633 at the time of an outbreak of plague.

The Thirty Years' War

In the Thirty Years' War of the early seventeenth century various European rulers fought over whether the areas they dominated should follow the Roman Catholic or the Protestant versions of Christianity. The sense of community was so strong that both sides regarded it as essential that all the Christians in each town should worship at the same church, and eventually it was settled that different areas should follow different practices: 'to each region its own religion'.

The plague spreads

At the end of the war many out-of-work soldiers were tramping back home across Europe, and with the breakdown of law and order and of basic hygienic practices, they were accompanied by large numbers of rats. The bubonic plague was a disease transmitted by fleas carried by the black rat. When people were bitten by the fleas they became infected with the bacillus *Yersinia pestis*. An early symptom of the plague was a painful swelling of lymph nodes, usually in the armpit and the groin; such swellings were

called 'buboes'. The plague caused virulent blood poisoning and the death rate was high.

The Black Death

In the children's rhyme the 'ring of roses' was the rash by which the plague was recognized, the 'pocketful of posies' was the bunch of flowers which people carried to ward off the smell of death and corruption, and after a sneezing fit, most of the sufferers did indeed fall down dead. In many cities wagons went round with the cry of 'bring out your dead,' of which there were so many that they were often dumped in a mass grave or plague pit. Between a third and a half of the population of Europe died of the Black Death in the fourteenth century.

The Plague in Oberammergau

The villagers of Oberammergau hoped to keep themselves free of the plague, which was decimating surrounding communities, by isolating themselves. They set watchmen on the roads, who lit bonfires so that even at night they could see anyone approaching the Village and keep them out, in case they were carrying the plague.

But one man, who had left Oberammergau to seek work elsewhere, wanted to return to see the bride he had recently married, and he knew a way to slip past the watchmen. The present which this home-comer brought with him to his native Village was the bubonic plague, and the burial registers show that in the next few months, out of a population of only about 600, 84 people died from it.

Luke 22:21–38

Jesus said, 'See, the one who betrays me is with me, and his hand is on the table. For the Son of Man is going as it has been determined, but woe to that one by whom he is betrayed!'

Then they began to ask one another, which one of them it could be who would do this. A dispute also arose among them as to which one of them was to be regarded as the greatest. But he said to them, 'The kings of the Gentiles lord it over them; and those in authority over them are called benefactors. But not so with you; rather the greatest among you must become like the youngest, and the leader like one who serves. For who is greater, the one who is at the table or the one who serves? Is it not the one at the table? But I am among you as one who serves.

'You are those who have stood by me in my trials; and I confer on you, just as my Father has conferred on me, a kingdom, so that you may eat and drink at my table in my kingdom, and you will sit on thrones judging the twelve tribes of Israel.

'Simon, Simon, listen! Satan has demanded to sift all of you like wheat, but I have prayed for you that your own faith may not fail; and you, when once you have turned back, strengthen your brothers.' And he said to him, 'Lord, I am ready to go with you to prison and to death!' Jesus said, 'I tell you, Peter, the cock will not crow this day, until you have denied three times that you know me.'

He said to them, 'When I sent you out without a purse, bag, or sandals, did you lack anything?' They said, 'No, not a thing.' He said to them, 'But now, the one who has a purse must take it, and likewise a bag. And the one who has no sword must sell his cloak and buy one. For I tell you, this scripture must be fulfilled in me, "And he was counted among the lawless"; and indeed what is written about me is being fulfilled.' They said, 'Lord, look, here are two swords.' He replied, 'It is enough.' (NRSV)

Prayer

'Saviour of the World'

Jesus, saviour of the world, come to us in your mercy: we look to you to save and help us.

By your cross and your life laid down you set your people free; we look to you to save and help us.

When they were ready to perish you saved your disciples: we look to you to come to our help.

In the greatness of your mercy loose us from our chains: forgive the sins of all your people.

Make yourself known as our saviour and mighty deliverer: save and help us that we may praise you.

Come now and dwell with us Lord Christ Jesus: hear our prayer and be with us always.

And when you come in your glory, make us to be one with you, and to share the life of your kingdom.

The Alternative Service Book 1980, p. 57,
possibly by Henry Allon (1818–92)

The Plague in London.

The Vow

The Village elders met in the Parish Church to pray about this crisis. The Church has since been rebuilt, but the crucifix before which they prayed still hangs to the right of the sanctuary in the present building. They made a vow, and although there is no record of the actual words they used, they certainly promised that, if the plague stopped in their Village, they would perform a Passion Play every ten years.

Nobody can force God to make a bargain with them: he is too great to need anything we can offer him. We shall never know whether the Oberammergau elders thought they were making a bargain with God, or whether it was a sincere promise of a gesture of thanksgiving if God would condescend to have pity on them. Neither can we know why God sometimes gives to some people exactly what they pray for, while to others he says 'No,' or 'Wait,' or 'I have something better to give you instead, though you may not recognize it yet as such.' Jesus himself, in the Garden of Gethsemane, prayed to be spared from drinking the cup of suffering, yet he had to drink it to the dregs.

An answered prayer

The prayer of the elders, however, was answered to the letter. From that day nobody else died of the plague in Oberammergau. The next year, 1634, the first Oberammergau Passion Play was performed in a meadow in front of the church.

From 1680 they decided to hold it at the beginning of each decade. With the exception of 1770, when it was forbidden, and 1940, during the Second World War, it has been produced every ten years ever since. The missing dates were compensated for by extra performances on the three hundredth and three hundred and fiftieth anniversaries of the first performance, in 1934 and 1984.

Bound by a vow

Some people are surprised that the villagers of today still feel bound by a vow made by their ancestors three and a half centuries ago. However, as the villagers see it, if ever they missed a performance, some terrible disaster would fall on them. This may appear to suggest that they believe in an impersonal law of cause and effect, or a vindictive God who needs to be placated.

It is amazing how many people believe that if something bad happens to them, God is punishing them. Or perhaps they think that if something happens which pleases them, then 'Somewhere in my youth or childhood I must have done something good!' Yet this is more like the Hindu or Buddhist belief in *karma* than the Christian idea of a loving heavenly Father who longs to pour out blessings on his children.

An act of worship

The villagers of Oberammergau know that they would not be alive today if God had not answered their forefathers' prayer, and they see the Passion Plays as an act of worship, showing their gratitude to the Father for his love. They believe that our relationship with God matters in our everyday life. Many communities have a ritual of re-enacting the events which mark the beginning of their life together. The Jewish Passover is one example, and the Oberammergau Passion Play is another.

At the service before the beginning of the 1990 season, the Cardinal from Munich told the villagers that the Play is a witness to their faith. In an age when many people break their vows of baptism, confirmation or marriage if they no longer feel like keeping them, it is refreshing to find a community which believes that the vow made by their ancestors is still solemnly binding on them.

The Palm Sunday procession.

Mark 14:32–42

They went to a place called Gethsemane; and Jesus said to his disciples, 'Sit here while I pray.' He took with him Peter and James and John, and began to be distressed and agitated. And he said to them, 'I am deeply grieved, even to death; remain here, and keep awake.' And going a little farther, he threw himself on the ground and prayed that, if it were possible, the hour might pass from him. He said, 'Abba, Father, for you all things are possible; remove this cup from me; yet, not what I want, but what you want.' He came and found them sleeping; and he said to Peter, 'Simon, are you asleep? Could you not keep awake one hour? Keep awake and pray that you may not come into the time of trial; the spirit indeed is willing, but the flesh is weak.'

And again he went away and prayed, saying the same words. And once more he came and found them sleeping, for their eyes were very heavy; and they did not know what to say to him. He came a third time and said to them, 'Are you still sleeping and taking your rest? Enough! The hour has come; the Son of Man is betrayed into the hands of sinners. Get up, let us be going. See, my betrayer is at hand.' (NRSV)

Prayer

And now we give you thanks because for our sins he was lifted high upon the cross that he might draw the whole world to himself; and by his suffering and death, became the source of eternal salvation for all who put their trust in him.

The Alternative Service Book 1980, p. 155, No. 9

Ettal and Unterammergau

Because of the shortage of accommodation in Oberammergau, many visitors to the Passion Play stay in hotels and guest houses in Ettal (four kilometres or two and a half miles up the Ammer River) or in Unterammergau (which is about the same distance downstream on the other side of Oberammergau) or in the other villages nearby. From these locations they are taken to the Play on regular shuttle buses.

Ettal Monastery

The priests of Oberammergau at the time of the vow came from the monastery at Ettal. It was one of them, Father Othmar Weis, who wrote the earliest surviving text of the Oberammergau Passion Play. This text was revised in 1860 by Joseph Alois Daisenberger, the parish priest of Oberammergau whose version is the basis of the one used today.

Ettal Monastery was founded in 1330 by Ludwig the Bavarian, an Emperor of the Holy Roman Empire, as a thanksgiving when he first set foot in Germany on returning from fierce battles near Rome. The original foundation was for twenty Benedictine monks and thirteen knights with their families. Ludwig brought with him a statue of the Virgin Mary in white Carara marble, carved by Tino di Camaino, which, in its niche behind the high altar, is still the focus of Ettal Abbey Church.

The church is round, in imitation of the Basilica of the Holy Sepulchre in Jerusalem. It was burnt down in 1744 and was rebuilt in Rococo style. Whereas Baroque architecture is flamboyantly ornamented with rather static figures symmetrically arranged on either side, Rococo is not symmetrical and the figures and statues are full of restless movement. Josef Schmuzer was the architect at Ettal, and the 52 metre (170 feet) high dome was painted by Johann Jakob Zeiller from Reutte. It shows the Holy Trinity of God the Father, Jesus his Son, and the Holy Spirit represented by a dove, praised by the disciples of St Benedict, the monks and nuns who follow the Rule of St Benedict in the Benedictine order and the other orders which have grown out of it.

The Ettal monastery was closed in 1803, but was given back to the Benedictines in 1900. The community now run a school, maintain a life of prayer and worship, brew beer and distil liqueurs. A shop by the gateway to the monastery sells Christian books and souvenirs.

Facilities in Ettal

Ettal has the same telephone dialling code as Oberammergau: 08822.

The Abbey: Open daily from 8 a.m. to 6 p.m. Admission free. Tel: 740.

Accommodation and travel: Verkehrsamt Gemeinde Ettal, Ammmergauer-Straße 8, D-82488 Ettal. Tel: 3534. Fax: 6399.

Bank: Sparkasse, open Monday to Wednesday and Friday 8 a.m. to 12 noon and 2–4 p.m.; Thursdays 8 a.m. to 12 noon and 2–5.30 p.m. Tel: 4888.

Mountain rescue: Tel: 6333.

Police station: The nearest is in Oberammergau. Tel: 6081.

Post office: Open Monday to Friday 9 a.m. to 12 noon and 2.30–5 p.m.; Saturday 9 a.m. to 12 noon. Tel: 4654.

Unterammergau

Unterammergau has an interesting church, built in 1709. Painted on the organ gallery is a stylized scene from the court of the Holy Roman Empire (which Voltaire described as neither holy, nor Roman, nor an empire!).

Facilities in Unterammergau

Unterammergau has the same telephone dialling code as Oberammergau: 08822.

Accommodation and travel: Verkehrsamt, Dorfstraße 23, D-82497 Unterammergau. Tel: 08822 6400. Fax: 7285. Mon-Fri 9am–12 noon

Banks: Kreissparkasse, Dorfstraße. Tel: 9204–0. Raiffeisenbank, Dorfstraße. Tel: 4224.

Mountain rescue: Tel: 1669.

Police station: The nearest is in Oberammergau. Tel: 6081.

Post office: In the Town Hall (*Rathaus*). Open Mondays to Fridays 9 a.m. to 12 noon and 2.30–5 p.m.; Saturdays 9 a.m. to 12 noon.

Railway Station: Tel: 3513.

Matthew 26:47–56

While Jesus was still speaking, Judas, one of the twelve, arrived; with him was a large crowd with swords and clubs, from the chief priests and the elders of the people. Now the betrayer had given them a sign, saying, 'The one I will kiss is the man; arrest him.' At once he came up to Jesus and said, 'Greetings, Rabbi!' and kissed him. Jesus said to him, 'Friend, do what you are here to do.' Then they came and laid hands on Jesus and arrested him. Suddenly, one of those with Jesus put his hand on his sword, drew it, and struck the slave of the high priest, cutting off his ear. Then Jesus said to him, 'Put your sword back into its place; for all who take the sword will perish by the sword. Do you think that I cannot appeal to my Father, and he will at once send me more than twelve legions of angels? But how then would the scriptures be fulfilled, which say it must happen in this way?'

At that hour Jesus said to the crowds, 'Have you come out with swords and clubs to arrest me as though I were a bandit? Day after day I sat in the temple teaching, and you did not arrest me. But all this has taken place, so that the scriptures of the prophets may be fulfilled.' Then all the disciples deserted him and fled. (NRSV)

Prayer

O Lord our God, grant us grace to desire you with our whole heart, that so desiring we may seek and find you, and so finding you, may love you, and loving you, may hate those sins from which you have redeemed us, through Jesus Christ our Lord. Amen.

St Anselm (1033–1109)

King Ludwig II

King Ludwig II of Bavaria was a nineteenth-century descendant of the Emperor Ludwig who founded Ettal. He played an important part in ensuring the survival of the Oberammergau Passion Play and is remembered with great affection throughout the region. On his birthday, 24 August, bonfires and fireworks are seen on many of the mountains.

At a time when many royal families were being overthrown by revolutions in Europe, the Bavarians retained a very feudal constitution within the German Federation.

Patron of the arts

King Ludwig II was a great patron of the arts, and he arranged for a private performance of the Oberammergau Passion Play, after which he gave each of the leading actors a silver spoon. Many of the passion plays at that time were very crude, with scenes such as whooping demons prancing around the dead Judas Iscariot, whose bowels gushing out were realistically represented with black sausages. So the passion plays were suppressed throughout the area as a harmful influence, with the exception of the Oberammergau Play, which was saved by the personal intervention of the King.

Statue of Christ

On a hillside above the Village Ludwig II erected a statue of Christ on the cross, with the Virgin Mary and the Apostle John, as his personal tribute to the Passion Play. At the time when it was erected it was the largest stone monument in Europe.

Perhaps King Ludwig chose a crucifix because he had personal experience of suffering (see below under 'Linderhof' and 'The Nymphenburg', pp. 21, 24).

Crucifixion

When we see a stone, metal or wooden crucifix, it is easy to forget that in crucifixion the Romans had acquired from the Persians the most painful method of execution ever invented. To see an actor in a Passion play hanging on a cross for about fifteen minutes brings many people for the first time to an understanding of what it cost Jesus to hang like that for three hours.

Crucifixion was used for slaves and rebels, and involved fixing the arms at such an angle that the sufferer could not breathe except by pushing himself up on the nail through his feet, in order to gasp a breath, and then sink down again, suspended by the nails through the wrists. After a few hours of this in the hot sun most criminals were too exhausted to continue, and died of suffocation. To ensure that they were dead, their legs were broken so that they could not lift themselves up any more. Jesus, however, had already died of a broken heart, so the soldiers did not need to break his legs. This fulfilled the prophecy, 'Not a bone of him shall be broken.'

Mark 14:53 – 15:1

They took Jesus to the high priest; and all the chief priests, the elders, and the scribes were assembled. Peter had followed him at a distance, right into the courtyard of the high priest; and he was sitting with the guards, warming himself at the fire.

Now the chief priests and the whole council were looking for testimony against Jesus to put him to death; but they found none. For many gave false testimony against him, and their testimony did not agree. Some stood up and gave false testimony against him, saying, 'We heard him say, "I will destroy this temple that is made with hands, and in three days I will build another, not made with hands."' But even on this point their testimony did not agree. Then the high priest stood up before them and asked Jesus, 'Have you no answer? What is it that they testify against you?' But he was silent and did not answer. Again the high priest asked him, 'Are you the Messiah, the Son of the Blessed One?' Jesus said, 'I am; and "you will see the Son of Man seated at the right hand of the Power," and "coming with the clouds of heaven."' Then the high priest tore his clothes and said, 'Why do we still need witnesses? You have heard his blasphemy! What is your decision?' All of them condemned him as deserving death. Some began to spit on him, to blindfold him, and to strike him, saying to him, 'Prophesy!' The guards also took him over and beat him.

While Peter was below in the courtyard, one of the servant-girls of the high priest came by. When she saw Peter warming himself, she stared at him and said, 'You also were with Jesus, the man from Nazareth.' But he denied it, saying, 'I do not know or understand what you are talking about.' And he went out into the forecourt. Then the cock crowed. And the servant-girl, on seeing him, began again to say to the bystanders, 'This man is one of them.' But again he denied it. Then after a little while the bystanders again said to Peter, 'Certainly you are one of them; for you are a Galilean.' But he began to curse, and he swore an oath, 'I do not know this man you are talking about.' At that moment the cock crowed for the second time. Then Peter remembered that Jesus had said to him, 'Before the cock crows twice, you will deny me three times.' And he broke down and wept.

As soon as it was morning, the chief priests held a consultation with the elders and scribes and the whole council. They bound Jesus, led him away, and handed him over to Pilate. (NRSV)

Prayer

O Lord God, our heavenly Father, regard, we pray, with your divine pity the pains of all your children; and grant that the passion of our Lord and his infinite love may make fruitful for good the tribulations of the innocent, the sufferings of the sick, and the sorrows of the bereaved; through him who suffered in our flesh and died for our sake, the same your Son our Saviour Jesus Christ. Amen.

Scottish Book of Common Prayer 1929 (modernised)

The Last Supper.

Neuschwanstein and Hohenschwangau

Few people visit Oberammergau without making a detour to visit the romantic castle of Neuschwanstein, famous from many movies such as *Chitty Chitty Bang-bang*, and its neighbour Hohenschwangau. We can also learn here some of the background to the origin and preservation of the Oberammergau Passion Play.

Hohenschwangau Castle

King Ludwig II lived some of the time in Munich and the rest of the time at Hohenschwangau, which is only twenty-four kilometres (fifteen miles) as the crow flies from Oberammergau.

This romantically situated castle rose to prominence in the twelfth century because of the German troubadour-knights known as *Minnesinger*. The troubadours who lived here were called the Schwangau knights, but they died out in the sixteenth century and the castle became a ruin. Ludwig II's father, King Maximilian II, bought it and restored it in 1832–6. It is richly furnished in the romantic style, and here Ludwig II entertained the composer Richard Wagner on several occasions.

Neuschwanstein Castle

Influenced by Wagner's operas and by the Romantic movement's fascination with the ancient German legends,

Ludwig II decided to build another castle within sight of Hohenschwangau 'in the true style of the ancient German knights' castles', as he said in a letter to Wagner in 1868. Neuschwanstein, the result, is more like a fairy-tale than any other castle in the world. Those who do not fancy the steep climb to visit it can travel most of the way to the castle in a horse and cart.

The throne room of Neuschwanstein is in Byzantine style with a thirteen-hundredweight (660-kilogram) chandelier in the shape of a Byzantine crown. The throne room has a fine tessellated pavement. There is no throne, as King Ludwig died before the castle was completed, but painted on the ceiling and reigning over the paintings of the twelve apostles and six canonized kings is the figure of Christ in glory.

The king's bed has a carved wooden canopy representing the gothic spires of German cathedrals, and there is a

1. Oberammergau from the Kofel

2. King Ludwig's crucifixion statue

3. A ceiling at Ettal Abbey

4. Madonna statue at Ettal Abbey

5. Neuschwanstein

6. The fountain at Linderhof

7. A ceiling at Linderhof

8. Peacock throne in Linderhof Pavilion

9. Starting young at the Oktoberfest, Munich

10. The oompah band

11. Toyseller statue, Oberammergau

12. Alpine wild flowers

13. The leap of faith

carving of the resurrection of Jesus at its foot. All the rooms are decorated with paintings of scenes from Wagner's operas. At the top of the castle is the sumptuous Singers' Hall, where the scene of Klingsor's magic forest was painted by Christian Jank, the scene painter at the Munich Royal Theatre, who was also responsible for most of the design of the castle and its furnishings. The kitchen at the lowest level has interesting equipment, and the view of the castle from Queen Mary's Bridge, suspended high above a gorge, is a delight for lovers of the romantic. King Ludwig II had lived in Neuschwanstein for less than a year before he died.

Information

Getting there: Schwanstein is near to Füssen on the B17 from Schongau, and the castles are on a side road turning off the B17 at Schwanstein.

Telephone contacts:
Dialling code: 08362.
Tourist Office,
Münchenerstraße 2, 87645
Schwangau. Tel: 8198-0.
Fax: 8198-25.
Hohenschwangau:
Tel: 81127. Fax: 81107.
Neuschwanstein: Tel: 81035.
Fax: 8990. Internet: http://
www.allgaeuschwaben.com/
sneuschwanstein.html

Opening hours for both castles: April to September: 8.30 a.m. to 5.30 p.m. daily. October to March: 10 a.m. to 4 p.m. daily. Admission fee, guided tours, coach park. Closed 1 November, 24, 25, 31 December and Shrove Tuesday.

The soldiers place a crown of thorns on Jesus' head.

John 18:28 – 19:16

Then they took Jesus from Caiaphas to Pilate's headquarters. It was early in the morning. They themselves did not enter the head-quarters, so as to avoid ritual defilement and to be able to eat the Passover. So Pilate went out to them and said, 'What accusation do you bring against this man?' They answered, 'If this man were not a criminal, we would not have handed him over to you.' Pilate said to them, 'Take him yourselves and judge him according to your law.' The Jews replied, 'We are not permitted to put anyone to death.' (This was to fulfill what Jesus had said when he indicated the kind of death he was to die.)

Then Pilate entered the headquarters again, summoned Jesus, and asked him, 'Are you the King of the Jews?' Jesus answered, 'Do you ask this on your own, or did others tell you about me?' Pilate replied, 'I am not a Jew, am I? Your own nation and the chief priests have handed you over to me. What have you done?' Jesus answered, 'My kingdom is not from this world. If my kingdom were from this world, my followers would be fighting to keep me from being handed over to the Jews. But as it is, my kingdom is not from here.'

Pilate asked him, 'So you are a king?' Jesus answered, 'You say that I am a king. For this I was born, and for this I came into the world, to testify to the truth. Everyone who belongs to the truth listens to my voice.' Pilate asked him, 'What is truth?'

After he had said this, he went out to the Jews again and told them, 'I find no case against him. But you have a custom that I release someone for you at the Passover. Do you want me to release for you the King of the Jews?' They shouted in reply, 'Not this man, but Barabbas!' Now Barabbas was a bandit.

Then Pilate took Jesus and had him flogged. And the soldiers wove a crown of thorns and put it on his head, and they dressed him in a purple robe. They kept coming up to him, saying, 'Hail, King of the Jews!' and striking him on the face. Pilate went out again and said to them, 'Look, I am bringing him out to you to let you know that I find no case against him.' So Jesus came out, wearing the crown of thorns and the purple robe. Pilate said to them, 'Here is the man!'

When the chief priests and the police saw him, they shouted, 'Crucify him! Crucify him!' Pilate said to them, 'Take him yourselves and crucify him; I find no case against him.' The Jews answered him, 'We have a law, and according to that law he ought to die because he has claimed to be the Son of God.'

Now when Pilate heard this, he was more afraid than ever. He entered his headquarters again and asked Jesus, 'Where are you from?' But Jesus gave him no answer. Pilate therefore said to him, 'Do you refuse to speak to me? Do you not know that I have power to release you, and power to crucify you?' Jesus answered him, 'You would have no power over me unless it had been given you from above; therefore the one who handed me over to you is guilty of a greater sin.'

From then on Pilate tried to release him, but the Jews cried out, 'If you release this man, you are no friend of the emperor. Everyone who claims to be a king sets himself against the emperor.' When Pilate heard these words, he brought Jesus outside and sat on the judge's bench at a place called The Stone Pavement, or in Hebrew Gabbatha. Now it was the day of Preparation for the Passover; and it was about noon. He said to the Jews, 'Here is your King!' They cried out, 'Away with him! Away with him! Crucify him!' Pilate asked them, 'Shall I crucify your King?' The chief priests answered, 'We have no king but the emperor.' Then he handed him over to them to be crucified. (NRSV)

Prayer

Jesus, poor, unknown and despised, have mercy on us, and let us not be ashamed to follow you. Jesus, accused, and wrongfully condemned, teach us to bear insults patiently, and let us not seek our own glory. Jesus, crowned with thorns and hailed in derision; buffeted, overwhelmed with injuries, griefs and humiliations; Jesus, hanging on the accursed tree, bowing the head, giving up the ghost, have mercy on us, and conform our whole lives to your spirit. Amen.

Adapted from John Wesley (1703–92)

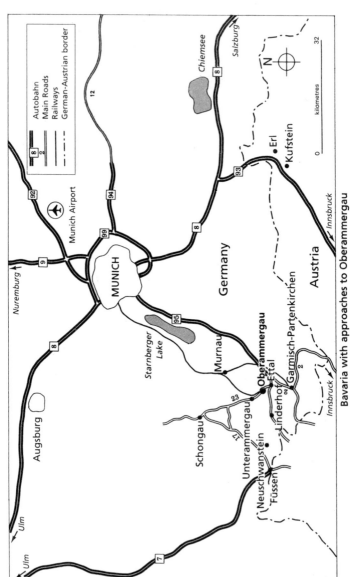

Bavaria with approaches to Oberammergau

Linderhof

Much nearer to Oberammergau (about ten kilometres or six miles away) is another of King Ludwig's castles, at Linderhof.

He became King in 1864 at the age of eighteen, following the death of his father, Maximilian II. His father's style of rule had been democratic, but Ludwig aimed to be an absolute monarch after the style of Louis XIV of France, the 'Sun King', whose statue stands in the entrance hall at Linderhof. He was inspired by the Petit Trianon Palace in Versailles to build a retreat at Linderhof where he could recreate the world of Wagner's *Tannhäuser*.

The interior

Visitors to Linderhof pass through the entrance hall and ascend the staircase to the Western Tapestry Room where the walls are, in fact, decorated with paintings made to look like tapestries.

Then the so-called 'Yellow Cabinet' is a room in the style of Louis XIV of France, with Meissen porcelain wall-light fittings.

In the Audience Chamber the King's throne stands behind a marble-topped desk, and the Lilac Cabinet beyond it also has fine Meissen porcelain.

The Bedchamber is modelled on the Versailles custom of the monarch receiving his court as he rose in the morning and when he went to bed, though in fact the shy Ludwig II lived a solitary life. The view from the window is of the water cascade in the grounds, and among all the sumptuous decoration don't miss the Meissen porcelain on either side of the window.

The Pink Cabinet contains a portrait of Madame du Barry, mistress of Louis XV. There is more Meissen in the Dining Room, with a marble reproduction of the famous Medici statue of Venus in the Uffizi Gallery in Florence.

Then follows the Blue Cabinet and the Eastern Tapestry Room, which has a Sevres porcelain peacock and a marble statue of the 'Three Graces'. Finally visitors pass through the Mirror Room, which must have looked wonderful when lit by candles.

The grounds

The grounds of Linderhof are beautifully laid out, with a fountain covered in gold leaf. The fountain normally plays every hour and rises high above the palace.

The newly reconstructed Hundinghütte represents the first act of Wagner's *Die Walküre*. The Moorish Kiosk and the

Moroccan House, were bought by the King after the 1867 Paris Exhibition ended and have been recreated in the grounds.

The Venus Grotto reproduces the first act of Wagner's *Tannhäuser*. There the King could sit in a gilded shell-shaped boat on a lake surrounded by artificial stalactites and stalagmites, next to the crystal-covered 'Lorelei Cliff', and dream that he was in the world of romantic fables. Special operatic performances were mounted in the grotto for the King.

Ludwig II was engaged in January 1867 to Princess Sophie, the daughter of Duke Maximilian of Bavaria, but the engagement was broken off in October the same year. The essential loneliness of his life is shown by the table in the Linderhof dining room, which can be raised through the floor from the kitchen below, already laden with food, so that the King did not have to see any of his servants when he dined alone.

Information

The telephone dialling code in Linderhof is 08822, the same as Oberammergau, Ettal and Unterammergau.

Getting there: Linderhof is on an unnumbered road signposted to Graswang, Linderhof and Reutte Tirol, turning off the road from Oberammergau to Ettal. There are buses to Linderhof from the Oberammergau railway station.

Information office: Staatliche Verwaltung, D-82488 Ettal-Linderhof. Tel: 3512. Fax: 3587.

Opening hours: October to March daily from 10 a.m. to 12.15 p.m. and 12.45–4 p.m.; April to September 9 a.m. to 12.15 p.m. and 12.45–5.30 p.m. Admission charge; guided tours by arrangement; coach park.

Jesus before Pontius Pilate.

Matthew 27:15–21

Now at the festival the governor was accustomed to release a prisoner for the crowd, anyone whom they wanted. At that time they had a notorious prisoner, called Jesus Barabbas. So after they had gathered, Pilate said to them, 'Whom do you want me to release for you, Jesus Barabbas or Jesus who is called the Messiah?' For he realized that it was out of jealousy that they had handed him over. While he was sitting on the judgment seat, his wife sent word to him, 'Have nothing to do with that innocent man, for today I have suffered a great deal because of a dream about him.' Now the chief priests and the elders persuaded the crowds to ask for Barabbas and to have Jesus killed. The governor again said to them, 'Which of the two do you want me to release for you?' And they said, 'Barabbas.' Pilate said to them, 'Then what should I do with Jesus who is called the Messiah?' All of them said, 'Let him be crucified!' Then he asked, 'Why, what evil has he done?' But they shouted all the more, 'Let him be crucified!'

So when Pilate saw that he could do nothing, but rather that a riot was beginning, he took some water and washed his hands before the crowd, saying, 'I am innocent of this man's blood; see to it yourselves.' Then the people as a whole answered, 'His blood be on us and on our children!' So he released Barabbas for them; and after flogging Jesus, he handed him over to be crucified.

Then the soldiers of the governor took Jesus into the governor's headquarters, and they gathered the whole cohort around him. They stripped him and put a scarlet robe on him, and after twisting some thorns into a crown, they put it on his head. They put a reed in his right hand and knelt before him and mocked him, saying, 'Hail, King of the Jews!' They spat on him, and took the reed and struck him on the head. After mocking him, they stripped him of the robe and put his own clothes on him. Then they led him away to crucify him. (NRSV)

Prayer

Lord Jesus, by the loneliness of your suffering on the cross, be near to all those who are desolate or in pain or sorrow at this time. Let your presence transform their loneliness into comfort, consolation, and fellowship with you, merciful Saviour. Amen.

Adapted from the Church of South India

Munich and the Nymphenburg

Many Passion Play visitors will pass through Munich on their way to or from Oberammergau. When King Ludwig II of Bavaria was not in one of the romantic castles which he himself had built, he liked to visit the Nymphenburg Palace in Munich, where he had been born.

The Palace's grounds

The Palace was built in 1663, and in its grounds are the carriage museum, a tiny Rococo gem of a palace called the Amelienburg, pavilions beside lakes at Budenburg and Pagodenburg, and the curious Magdalen Chapel. Next to the grounds of the palace are the Botanical Gardens.

The Palace's interior

Inside the Nymphenburg Palace are spacious and well-furnished rooms. In one of these rooms is the 'Gallery of Beauties'. Painted on the orders of King Ludwig I, the gallery consists of portraits of all the most beautiful women of his day. Most of them he had never set eyes on, but a few of them were his mistresses, whom the Queen had to entertain in the palace when they visited Munich.

The most notorious of these was an Irish adventuress who travelled as a Spanish dancer under the name of Lola Montez. She gained such power over the King that eventually the people compelled him to banish her from the kingdom. It is said that they were so relieved when she left that they saw no need for a revolution in Bavaria, when the rest of Europe was dethroning its kings.

Munich

Munich's German name, *München*, comes from the word for 'monks', as the city was founded on the site of a monastery. The dancing copper figures on the Glockenspiel Tower of the Town Hall in the Marienplatz move at 11 a.m. and noon daily, and from May until October they also move at 5 p.m. After the 11 a.m. chime a walking tour of the city begins from the foot of the Glockenspiel, with an English-speaking guide.

A tour of the city

If visitors prefer to walk alone, they can pass from the Marienplatz to St Peter's Church (see the beginning of this book for opening times of churches), dating from the eleventh century, with its eight clock-faces on the tower; to the Food Market; to the Holy Ghost Church (1392); to the Old Town Hall (1474); and to one of the beer cellars, such as the Hofbräuhaus.

Then, passing the National Theatre, the home of the Bavarian State Opera, a visit can be paid to the Residence, including its museum, more theatres (where Mozart's *Idomeneo* had its first performance) and the crown jewels in the Treasury (see below for opening times).

Opposite the Residence is the Theatiner Church (1633–88), and from there a tour can pass on to the Frauenkirche (St Mary's, Munich's cathedral, dating from 1488), whose onion-shaped towers set the pattern for many of the churches of Bavaria.

If time permits, St Michael's Church (1597), the gloriously rococo Asam Church (1746) and the National Museum are also worth visiting.

The Oktoberfest

The Oktoberfest is a celebration each September, ending on the first Sunday in October. The Theresienwiese is covered with hundreds of food stalls and beer tents and one of Europe's most extensive funfairs. Especially strong beer is drunk from litre glasses, ten or twelve of which the waitresses can carry at one time.

Aloïs

The shops sell puppets of Aloïs, a legendary Munich railway station porter. He went to heaven when he died, and was allowed a special robe in the blue-and-white diamond pattern of the Bavarian royal arms. But finding that there was no Bavarian beer in heaven, he sang 'Alleluia!' so loudly that God sent him down to the Munich Parliament to ask for a supply to be laid on. But it is said that he went back to his *Stammtisch*, the special table in one of the beer cellars where he and his cronies used to meet, and he has not yet delivered the message!

Beer Gardens

In fine weather it is pleasant to visit one of the Beer Gardens under the horse-chestnut trees in the parks. It is said that Germans drink their beer from a *Stein* with a lid in order to stop the conkers falling into the beer!

The death of Ludwig II

On 10 June 1886 King Ludwig II was declared insane by his physicians and was deposed from his throne. On 12 June, accompanied by his psychiatrist, the King was taken from Neuschwanstein to the Berg Palace, south west of Munich, and on 13 June he and the psychiatrist were found drowned in a few feet of water in the nearby Starnberger Lake.

The true circumstances of this suspicious death may never be known, but some people believe that, although undoubtedly eccentric, the King was never mad, and was deposed and then murdered for political reasons. Within weeks of his death the royal family decided that they could not maintain the castles he had built, and handed them all over to the state.

How to get around in Munich

You can buy an all-day travel pass (*Tageskarte*) valid on the trams and buses or on the S-bahn or U-bahn (partially underground) in advance from the machines at the stations, or from a shop with the white-and-green 'K' symbol. It needs to be validated (only once) by putting it in a machine at a station or on a tram or bus.

Most tram and bus routes converge at the Hauptbahnhof, the main railway station. There take the U-bahn (route U1) to Rotkreuzplatz, then change to tram 12 to the Nymphenburg. To get to the Oktoberfest take route U4 or U5 from the Hauptbahnhof to the Theresienwiese.

Information

The telephone dialling code from outside Munich is 089 for all Munich numbers.

For information on Upper Bavaria write to Tourismusverband, München-Oberbayern e.V., Postfach 60 03 20, D-81203 München, Germany. Tel: 089 8292 18-0. Fax: 18-28. Brochures 18-30.

When in Munich visit the Fremdenverkehrsamt, Hauptbahnhof (main railway station) Bayerstraße (southern) exit. Open Monday to Saturday 9 a.m. to 8 p.m.; Sundays 10 a.m. to 6 p.m. Tel: 23330-256 or 257.

The Residence, the Residence Museum and the Treasury: Open Tuesday to Sunday 10 a.m. to 4.30 p.m. Closed Mondays. Admission charge. No coach park. Tel: 290671. Fax: 2906 7225.

The Nymphenburg Palace: Open Tuesday to Sunday 9 a.m. to 12.30 p.m., 1.30–5 p.m. April to September, but closing at 4 p.m. in winter. Closed Mondays. Admission charge, guided tours, coach park, café in the park. Information: Schloß-und Garten-verwaltung, Schloß Nymphenburg, Eingang 1, D–80638 München. Tel: 17 90 86 68. Fax: 17 90 81 54.

Luke 23:26–32

As they led Jesus away, they seized a man, Simon of Cyrene, who was coming from the country, and they laid the cross on him, and made him carry it behind Jesus. A great number of the people followed him, and among them were women who were beating their breasts and wailing for him. But Jesus turned to them and said, 'Daughters of Jerusalem, do not weep for me, but weep for yourselves and for your children. For the days are surely coming when they will say, "Blessed are the barren, and the wombs that never bore, and the breasts that never nursed." Then they will begin to say to the mountains, "Fall on us"; and to the hills, "Cover us." For if they do this when the wood is green, what will happen when it is dry?' Two others also, who were criminals, were led away to be put to death with him. (NRSV)

Prayer

We praise you, O God, because through Christ you have given us the hope of a glorious resurrection; so that, although death comes to us all, yet we rejoice in the promise of eternal life; for to your faithful people life is changed, not taken away; and when our mortal flesh is laid aside, an everlasting dwelling place is made ready for us in heaven.

Adapted from *The Roman Missal*

Pilate washes his hands.

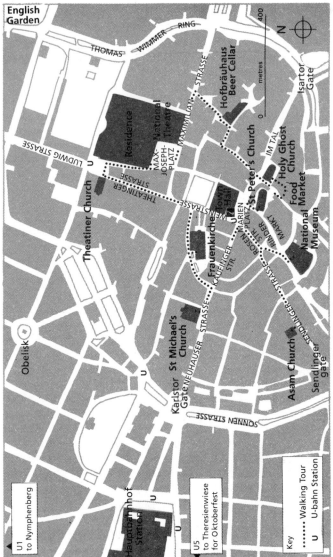

Munich with a walking tour

Bavaria, the Tyrol and the Chiemsee

Visitors are attracted to this part of Germany and Austria not only by the historic towns and cities but also by the natural beauty of the mountains, valleys and lakes. If you take a gentle stroll through the countryside you will enjoy constantly changing vistas of delightful scenery.

Many of the mountains have a *Sesselbahn* (chair-lift) or a *Seilbahn* (cabin cable car), some of which, as well as taking skiers to the tops of the ski runs in winter, will, in summer, take passengers to the beginning of walks along well-marked mountain footpaths, where the route can be chosen to be as strenuous or as easy as the walker requires.

Alpine flowers

In the spring and summer the Alpine flowers grow in profusion, forming a carpet of colour across the mountains. There are so many species that an expert or a good book is needed to identify them. And in some places there are special gardens where nearly every known species is grown. Even in winter the hardy Edelweiss can be found in sheltered spots amidst the snow.

Visitors are asked not to pick the wild flowers, as it prevents others from enjoying them, and there is always a risk that a species might die out.

Lakes

The mountain valleys were carved into shape by the glaciers of the last ice age. When it retreated, each glacier left a moraine of stones across the valley floor at the furthest point to which it had carried them. Many of these moraines formed natural dams to the rivers which still flow down from the mountains, and in many places a lake mirrors the peaks of the mountains above.

Maypoles

Many local villages have a blue-and-white maypole at their centre, decorated with symbols of all the trades plied there, to inform passing youths what apprenticeships may be available. If it is taken down for repainting it may be stolen by a rival village, and it can only be bought back at the cost of a large quantity of beer!

Herrenchiemsee

The largest lake in Bavaria is the Chiemsee (82 sq. km.), between Munich and Salzburg. In the middle of this is the

Herrenchiemsee island, where King Ludwig II built a castle modelled on the central portion of Versailles. It was never finished, but parts of it are sumptuously furnished. Its curiosities include the King's bath, and the workings of the 'vanishing table', which takes so long to wind up from the kitchen that the food would have been cold by the time the King ate it!

Information

Staadliche Verwaltung, Altes Schloß 3, 83209 Herrenchiemsee. Tel: 08051 3069. Fax: 3069 or 64646.

Opening hours and guided tours: April to September, 9 a.m. to 5 p.m.; the rest of the year 10 a.m. to 4 p.m. Admission charge.

Fraueninsel

On the smaller Fraueninsel island is a Benedictine convent, probably founded in the year 766, with the relics of the Blessed Irmengard, an abbess of the Abbey of Frauenchiemsee and a great grand-daughter of the Emperor Charlemagne. She died young on 16 July 866.

Abbey opening hours: May to October, 11 a.m. to 6 p.m. Tel: 08054 903912. Fax: 903917.

Boats on the Chiemsee

The fleet of boats taking visitors to these islands includes a paddle-steamer which has been plying the lake since 1926.

Prien and Stock, the ports from which the Chiemsee steamers depart, can be reached by train on the Munich-Salzburg line or by taking the Bernau exit from the Munich-Salzburg Autobahn.

Boat information:
Chiemsee-Schiffahrt, Ludwig Feßler, D-83210 Prien am Chiemsee, Postfach 21. Tel: 08051 1510.

General information about the Chiemsee

Verkehrsverband Chiemsee e.V., Rathausstraße 11, D-83209 Prien am Chiemsee. Tel: 08051 2280 and 6905-35. Fax: 61097.

A thought to ponder

Many people have said that they feel nearer to God in the mountains. Not literally, of course, for we know that heaven is not a place above the clouds, but the state of being with God, and God is everywhere. But in the pure mountain air the grandeur of what God has created can be seen, and the puny size of our best efforts in comparison. It helps us to see ourselves in perspective and our total dependence on God's care. In the silence we can pray without distractions. It was no accident that it was on a high mountain that Jesus was transfigured before his disciples and they recognized him as the Son of God. Immediately afterwards, however, they had to descend from the mountains to the busy life of the plain, to a sick boy and an unbelieving crowd. Can our 'mountain-top experiences' – even those which occur in a theatre, a concert hall or a library – inspire and strengthen us to show practical love to our neighbours when we come back down to earth?

Jesus falls on the way of the cross.

Package or Pilgrimage?

Why do people visit Oberammergau? Is it fair to call this book *Every Pilgrim's Guide to Oberammergau* when many people go there simply for a holiday?

Friendliness

Visitors go to the Alpine region for many reasons. The friendliness of the people, in their *lederhosen* shorts or *dirndl* dresses, and the thigh-slapping *Schuhplattler* dances, always bring a sense of enjoyment. The ample and jolly welcome of the hostess of 'Tini's Restaurant' as she serves the beer, and the cheerful yodeller who entertains there, could be repeated in many tourists' recollections of similar establishments in other Alpine towns. With luck, the town's 'oompah band' may enliven the day.

Greetings

The people of the mountains seem to be naturally religious, though here as elsewhere things are changing. However, everywhere in the region, even now, you will be greeted by total strangers with the phrase *Grüss Gott*, meaning roughly,

Simon of Cyrene is forced to carry Jesus' cross.

'Greetings in the name of God,' and you will be expected to reply with the same words. For those who do not already speak it, there are some hints at the end of this book about learning a few phrases of German. The dialect farewell, *Pfüat di Gott* (*Pfüat eich Gott*, if you are being formal or are speaking to more than one person), is even harder to translate, but like the English word 'Goodbye', it means something like 'God be with you, protect you and guide you.'

Growing fame

For the first 200 years the villagers of Oberammergau performed the Passion Play for their own benefit, in fulfilment of the vow, and to the glory of God. Then the railway was built as far as Weilheim, from where a coach and horses could be hired to drag travellers up the muddy and often dangerous tracks to the top of the Ammer Valley. The road was not metalled until 1889, but the railway was extended to Murnau in 1880, and then to Garmisch Partenkirchen by 1890. Now most visitors come by road in diesel coaches which fill the streets of the Village on 'arrival and departure days'.

Thomas Cook

Thomas Cook was a Baptist in Leicester, England, who had the idea of performing an act of Christian service to his poorer neighbours by hiring a train to take them to a Temperance rally at Loughborough. Very soon he was taking groups further afield for 'Cook's Tours', and modern tourism was born. In 1869 he took his first party of pilgrims to the Holy Land, and in 1871 he organized the first English group to visit Oberammergau.

Fashionable

Individual travellers had already reported their impressions of Oberammergau's Passion Play in the London *Times*, and in 1871 the Prince of Wales (the future King Edward VII of England) and his wife visited the Play, vainly attempting to do so incognito.

With this example, a visit to Oberammergau became fashionable, and already in 1910 almost 5,000 people at a time were coming in and out for a total of fifty-six performances. Still in 1990 over 60% of the 450,000 visitors were from countries of the English-speaking world.

Package tours

Sadly, some of the visitors come as part of a package tour of Europe, and without suitable preparation they are baffled by the long and stately performance, when their normal experience of drama has been half-hour 'soaps' on television. Some people's ignorance about the Christian faith is staggering: one man was heard to ask about Jesus, during

33

the lunch interval, 'They're not going to kill him, are they?'

Pilgrims

Travellers have been described as those who don't know where they are going, and tourists have been called those who don't know where they have been. In that case pilgrims are those who set out for a place where they can meet God, and find that God has been with them throughout the journey.

This book aims to turn a package tour into a pilgrimage.

Whatever hardships the pilgrims of the Middle Ages had to bear, and however much it cost them, they travelled with the expectation of receiving some spiritual benefit, and most of them did. While sitting and waiting for a Passion Play to begin, if not before, it is good to pray for all who take part, for all the spectators, and for yourself, that all may come away with a deeper love for God and a stronger desire to love and serve their neighbours.

Veronica wipes the face of Jesus.

Hebrews 11:13–19

The heroes of the past died in faith without having received the promises. They welcomed what was promised, like people seeing their destination from far away. They admitted that they were strangers and pilgrims on earth, for people who speak in this way make it clear that they are seeking a homeland. If they had been thinking of the land that they had left behind, they would have had opportunity to return. As it is, they long for a better country, that is, a heavenly one. So God is not ashamed to be called their God; in fact he has prepared a city for them to live in.

By faith Abraham, when God tested him, offered up his son Isaac. God had promised Abraham that he would only have descendants through Isaac, yet he was willing to offer his only son back to God. He believed that God is able even to raise someone from the dead – and in a manner of speaking, he did receive him back from death.

Prayer

Lord God, may we love your creation, all the earth and every grain of sand in it. May we love every leaf, every ray of your light. May we love the animals. Let us not trouble them; let us not harass them, let us not deprive them of their well-being, let us not work against your intent. We acknowledge that to you all is like an ocean, all is flowing and blending, and that to withhold love from anything in your universe is to withhold that same love from you.

Adapted from *The Brothers Karamazov*
by Feodor Dostoevsky (1821–81)

The English Language Church Welcome Centre

One of the most satisfying experiences for a Christian minister is to work with people whose faith is being deepened.

The history of the Centre

Inter-Church Travel, which had been formed to provide ecumenical pilgrimages in the 1950s, received, quite unexpectedly, 10,000 bookings for the 1960 Passion Play. They regarded it as important to bring pilgrims of different denominations together to help them to view the Play as a spiritual experience.

An Anglican chaplain had been provided by the SPG (The Society for the Propagation of the Gospel) in the tiny Lutheran Church since 1890. The Reverend Arthur Payton, then managing director of Inter-Church Travel, agreed with SPG and the Bishop of Fulham, then responsible for Europe, to provide an Ecumenical Centre in 1960 in the Turnhalle, separate from the chaplaincy; in 1970 he was asked to take responsibility for the chapaincy also. In 1967 Inter-Church Travel was taken over by Thomas Cook Ltd, who sold it to Saga Ltd in the mid-1980s.

Involving much hard work by many caring and spiritual people, teams of ministers have gone to Oberammergau for two weeks at a time during the season to staff the centre. The Roman Catholic priest of the Village has kindly allowed the parish hall on the corner of Hillernstraße and Herkul.-Schwaiger-Straße to be used for the centre, and for the year 2000 it has been completely rebuilt.

Although it is some distance from the centre of the Village it is well signposted. It has provided a comfortable welcome for those who wish to visit it. In the year 2000 a centre with a new name but on similar lines will be sponsored by the Council of Churches in Britain and Ireland and administered by the Diocese of Europe.

The Team

The Team of ministers at the Welcome Centre always includes a catholic priest, and tries to keep a balance of denominations and of male and female ministers.

The ministry of the Team has focused on waiting in all weathers at the coach park to board each bus as it arrives, provided that the passengers understand English. The Team have then welcomed them to the Village and have wished them a wonderful visit to the Play. For some visitors, for whom this was their only contact with the Team, just the friendly greeting in their own language helped them to feel among friends.

Preparatory talks

The Team have also invited the people whom they have met on the buses, and any others who read the widely distibuted leaflets, (once they had settled into their accommodation and had eaten a meal) to attend a preparatory talk about the Play and a short act of devotion in the Centre on the evening before the Play was performed.

The preparatory talks have sometimes been attended by more than 200 people at a time. Each speaker approaches the talk in his or her own way, and no two are the same, but visitors have often said that these meetings have been second only to the Play itself as a high point of the visit, changing the mood of a mostly secular holiday into one of spiritual expectation about the Play.

Services

The Roman Catholic priest on the Team has also said Mass in the Parish Church in English, concelebrating with other visiting priests as required, immediately after the Play. The other members of the Team have also led services – in 2000, the Anglican–Lutheran Holy Communion (open to all Christians) after the Play will be in the Lutheran Church – and have welcomed visiting clergy to use the centre for worship services for their own groups.

All the Team have made themselves available to give counselling to those who wanted it, and sacramental absolution has been given when required. The reward that the volunteer Team members received was when visitors sought them out after the Play to tell them what their reactions had been.

A rewarding ministry

Many visitors have commented that the Team, who had seldom met each other before, quickly became firm friends and so obviously enjoyed working together. This is a witness to and a foretaste of the future unity of the Church. As one American visitor commented, 'We're all supporting the same football team – we're just shouting for different parts of the pitch!' To be on the staff of the Centre, although it is hard work, is a rewarding and enjoyable ministry.

John 17:20–23

Jesus prayed to his Father, saying, 'I ask not only on behalf of these disciples here, but also on behalf of those who will believe in me through their word, that they may all be one. As you, Father, are in me and I am in you, may they also be in us, so that the world may believe that you have sent me. The glory that you have given me I have given them, so that they may be one, as we are one, I in them and you in me, that they may become completely one, so that the world may know that you have sent me and have loved them even as you have loved me.' (NRSV)

Prayer

God the Father of all, your Church is not catholic because we do not seek to comprehend within one family all the ways in which you are understood. Forgive us and make us truly catholic. Lord, have mercy. **Lord, have mercy.**

God the Son who died for all, your Church is not evangelical because the gospel of your universal love is concealed by our narrowness and prejudice. Forgive us and make us truly evangelical. Christ, have mercy. **Christ, have mercy.**

God the Spirit, you work through all and are in all. Your Church is not charismatic because we have pretended that our gifts are better than other people's, and have not made them subservient to the best gift of love. Forgive us and make us truly charismatic. Lord, have mercy. **Lord, have mercy.**

Michael Counsell in *More Prayers for Sundays*

Bahnhofstraße A-1
Bärenbadstraße D-2
Daisenbergerstraße C-2
Devrientweg B-1
Dorfplatz B-1
Dorfstrasse B-1
Eugen-Papst-Straße B-1
Ettaler Straße C-1
Faistenmantelgasse C-1
Feldiglgasse B-1
Herkul.-Schwaiger-Straße C-2
Hillernstraße C-2
Himmelreich E-1
Hubertusstraße C-3
In der Breitenau C-1
König-Ludwig-Straße B-2
Laberweg C-3

Latschenkopfstraße D-2
Kreuzweg C-2
Leupoldstraße C-2
Ludwig-Lang-Straße C-2
Malensteinweg B-3
Michael-Diemer-Straße D-2
Moosgasse A-1
Ottmar-Weiß-Straße B-1
Passionswiese B-1
Rainenbichl D-3
Rottenbucherstraße A-1
Ruedererweg C-3
Schnitzlergasse C-2
St.-Lukas-Straße C-1
Theaterstraße B-1
Waldschmidtstraße C-3
Warbergerstraße C-1

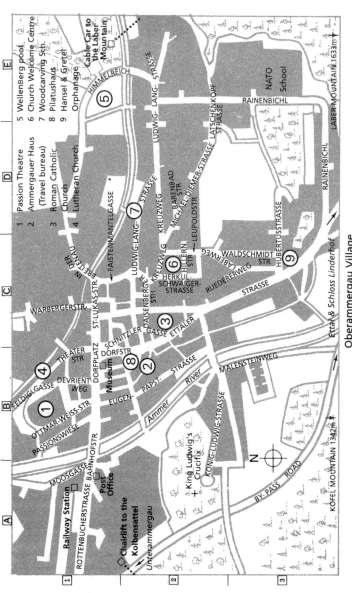

1 Passion Theatre
2 Ammergauer Haus (Travel bureau)
3 Roman Catholic Church
4 Lutheran Church
5 Wellenberg pool
6 Church Welcome Centre
7 Woodcarving Sch.
8 Pilatushaus
9 Hansel & Gretel Orphanage

Oberammergau Village

Accommodation

Traditionally, visitors to Oberammergau were accommodated in the homes of the villagers, and the visitors would joyfully exchange the information that they were staying with the High Priest Caiaphas or the Apostle Peter, since most households in the Village would have at least one family member with a part in the Play.

However, more and more guest houses and hotels have opened in recent times, at least in Passion Play years, to meet the growing demand. Previously the coaches were met by teenage lads with wheelbarrows, who took the visitors' suitcases to their accommodation, but in recent years they have been replaced by a fleet of buses.

Because of the pressure on space, nobody can stay in the Village during the Passion Play for more than two nights, and only for one if they are seeing the Play on a Sunday. Most

Moses lifts up the bronze serpent in the wilderness.

A busy season!

Many of the villagers have to work in three ways during the Play season:

- They continue to do the work which employs them during the other nine years.
- They are involved in the Play: between 2,000 and 2,500 out of a population of about 5,000 are either on stage at some point or involved behind the scenes.
- In their own homes or helping in the hotels, guest houses and restaurants, they have to feed 5,000 visitors for each performance, change the sheets and clean their rooms after they have left.

Play tickets are sold as part of an 'Arrangement' including accommodation, though Saturday's performances are intended for those who are not staying in the Village.

Acting is emotionally draining. So is being nice to people whom they have never seen before, who do not speak the same language, and who may be irritable after a tiring journey. It is small wonder that the entire population of Oberammergau is exhausted by the end of the season. For them, producing the Passion Play every ten years is a real sacrifice. It would be easier if they catered for half as many visitors every five years. But, they reply, 'That was not what we vowed.'

Isaiah 52:13 – 53:12

See, my servant shall prosper; he shall be exalted and lifted up, and shall be very high. Just as there were many who were astonished at him – so marred was his appearance, beyond human semblance, and his form beyond that of mortals – so he shall startle many nations; kings shall shut their mouths because of him; for that which had not been told them they shall see, and that which they had not heard they shall contemplate.

Who has believed what we have heard? And to whom has the arm of the Lord been revealed? For he grew up before him like a young plant, and like a root out of dry ground; he had no form or majesty that we should look at him, nothing in his appearance that we should desire him. He was despised and rejected by others; a man of suffering and acquainted with infirmity; and as one from whom others hide their faces he was despised, and we held him of no account. →

Surely he has borne our infirmities and carried our diseases; yet we accounted him stricken, struck down by God, and afflicted. But he was wounded for our transgressions, crushed for our iniquities; upon him was the punishment that made us whole, and by his bruises we are healed. All we like sheep have gone astray; we have all turned to our own way, and the Lord has laid on him the iniquity of us all. He was oppressed, and he was afflicted, yet he did not open his mouth; like a lamb that is led to the slaughter, and like a sheep that before its shearers is silent, so he did not open his mouth. By a perversion of justice he was taken away. Who could have imagined his future? For he was cut off from the land of the living, stricken for the transgression of my people. They made his grave with the wicked and his tomb with the rich, although he had done no violence, and there was no deceit in his mouth.

Yet it was the will of the Lord to crush him with pain. When you make his life an offering for sin, he shall see his offspring, and shall prolong his days; through him the will of the Lord shall prosper. Out of his anguish he shall see light; he shall find satisfaction through his knowledge. The righteous one, my servant, shall make many righteous, and he shall bear their iniquities. Therefore I will allot him a portion with the great, and he shall divide the spoil with the strong; because he poured out himself to death, and was numbered with the transgressors; yet he bore the sin of many, and made intercession for the transgressors. (NRSV)

Prayer

Almighty God, whose most dear Son went not up to joy but first he suffered pain, and entered not into glory before he was crucified: mercifully grant that we, walking in the way of the cross, may find it none other than the way of life and peace; through Jesus Christ our Lord. Amen.

William Reed Huntingdon (1838–1909)

Money-Making or Ministry?

If it is so tiring, why do the people of Oberammergau continue to produce the Play every ten years? Do they do it just to become rich?

Are the actors paid?

It is commonly said that none of the actors at Oberammergau is paid. That is not strictly true, since they are all compensated for loss of earnings. And in 1990, for the first time, those playing the principal characters, who have to give up their regular employment for the season, were paid a salary, amid much head-shaking from the older villagers at this departure from tradition. So nobody becomes rich by taking part in the Play.

Hard work

Providing food and accommodation for guests and making and selling souvenirs are hard and time-consuming work, and probably nobody would do it unless they expected to make some profit out of it. These things are lucrative in Passion Play years, and some of that income spreads to other villagers also by way of trade.

In the nine years between Passion Plays, however,

Jesus is stripped of his clothes.

although Oberammergau works hard to attract tourists to come for other reasons, many restaurants and guest-houses have to close, and some people live off their savings. The houses in the Village look comfortable and prosperous, but then, all Germans are accustomed to spending a higher proportion of their income on their homes than people in some other countries think desirable or necessary.

Municipal projects

Any profit on the Passion Play, from the difference between the sale of tickets and the costs of the production, is always spent on municipal projects of benefit to residents and visitors alike.

A superb complex of swimming pools, with an exciting wave machine, is still being developed. Cable cars run up and down the mountains. The Ammergauer Haus is a comfortable hall which serves as an administrative centre for community meetings, and it hosted an exhibition in 1990.

The Passion Theatre

Since 1990 the Passion Theatre has been fully renovated, with comfortable seats, under-floor heating, stage machinery and a new external facade, with up-to-date fire-prevention and first-aid facilities, all paid for out of the profit from the Play.

Scandal

However, in 1990 there was a scandal which, the villagers felt, might unjustly tarnish their good name. It is alleged that a certain man, not a native of Oberammergau, bought one of the hotels in the Village and offered accommodation in it coupled with a Play ticket – except that he did not have any tickets.

Several tour operators seem not to have appreciated that the only way to buy Play tickets is through the Village authorities, and unfortunate visitors were arriving all through the season thinking that they had Play tickets, only to discover that they had none.

The Village authorities recommended them to take the hotelier to court, because it was in fact no fault of the Village, although they were being blamed. The few remaining tickets were as scarce as gold dust. The only hope for those without tickets was to form a line outside the Theatre from four or five in the morning, and even then most of them could not obtain any.

Sacrifices

In spite of the great sacrifices which the villagers make – sacrifices of time, convenience and effort – they are much criticized for being too commercially minded. It would be more charitable to think of the great service they perform in enabling 5,000 visitors – one for every resident of the Village, five times a week – to share in their act of worship to Almighty God, and in bringing before us, in a way that we may never before have understood, the great love of Jesus in sacrificing his life so that we might be forgiven. How anyone can complain of discomfort, or criticize or hate others after seeing such a Play, defies comprehension.

Mark 10:32–45

They were on the road, going up to Jerusalem, and Jesus was walking ahead of them; they were amazed, and those who followed were afraid. He took the twelve aside again and began to tell them what was to happen to him, saying, 'See, we are going up to Jerusalem, and the Son of Man will be handed over to the chief priests and the scribes, and they will condemn him to death; then they will hand him over to the Gentiles; they will mock him, and spit upon him, and flog him, and kill him; and after three days he will rise again.'

James and John, the sons of Zebedee, came forward to him and said to him, 'Teacher, we want you to do for us whatever we ask of you.' And he said to them, 'What is it you want me to do for you?' And they said to him, 'Grant us to sit, one at your right hand and one at your left, in your glory.' But Jesus said to them, 'You do not know what you are asking. Are you able to drink the cup that I drink, or be baptized with the baptism that I am baptized with?' They replied, 'We are able.' Then Jesus said to them, 'The cup that I drink you will drink; and with the baptism with which I am baptized, you will be baptized; but to sit at my right hand or at my left is not mine to grant, but it is for those for whom it has been prepared.'

When the ten heard this, they began to be angry with James and John. So Jesus called them and said to them, 'You know that among the Gentiles those whom they recognize as their rulers lord it over them, and their great ones are tyrants over them. But it is not so among you; but whoever wishes to become great among you must be your servant, and whoever wishes to be first among you must be slave of all. For the Son of Man came not to be served but to serve, and to give his life a ransom for many.' (NRSV)

Prayer

Almighty and everliving God, in your tender love for the human race you sent your Son our Saviour Jesus Christ to take upon him our nature, and to suffer death upon the cross, giving us the example of his great humility: Mercifully grant that we may walk in the way of his suffering, and also share in his resurrection; through Jesus Christ our Lord, who lives and reigns with you and the Holy Spirit, one God, for ever and ever. Amen.

US Book of Common Prayer 1979,
from the Gelasian Sacramentary

Abraham and Isaac: the son carries the wood for his own sacrifice.

Still a Village

Although it is unlike anywhere else on earth, Oberammergau is still a village. At all available hours throughout the Play season, the hay is still brought in to feed the cows through the winter. The cowsheds stand in the middle of the village, smelling just the same as every other cowshed, and much like the stable where the baby Jesus was born.

No stage make-up is used, so everyone with a part in the Play has to grow their hair to the appropriate length. Thus you will find the postman cycling round with a full patriarchal beard and flowing locks, and among the younger children it is hard to tell the boys from the girls. There is something very moving in seeing 'Jesus' riding past on a green bicycle, or in being served in a shop by 'St Peter'.

More than human

It helps us to remember that Jesus was apparently just like all the other villagers of his time. 'Is not this the carpenter's son?' asked the people of Nazareth (Matthew 13:55). 'He had no form or comeliness that we should admire him' (Isaiah 53:2). It was only as his disciples came to know him closely and saw that the great love in his heart for everyone, including the outcast and despised, resembled the love of God the Father whom he talked of, that they began to realise that this seemingly ordinary man was somebody special, and wondered whether perhaps he might be more than merely human. Many people today admire Jesus as a man and a prophet, but not until they have known him for a long time as a friend are they ready to acknowledge him by any grander title. Surely he accepts that?

Blood on his hands

In 1990 I went to hire a bicycle from one of the carpenters of Oberammergau at his workshop in the Fendtgasse. As he adjusted the saddle height for me, I noticed that his brawny hands were stained red. Alarmed that he had cut himself, I asked if that was his blood on his hands. 'No,' he replied, with a wry smile. 'That is the blood of Christ – I'm the soldier who nails him to the cross!' I knew, and he knew that I knew, that it was only paint. But what effect is it going to have on a man to know that, even if only symbolically, he has the blood of Christ on his hands five times a week for five months?

Saint and sinner

The villagers of Oberammergau would be the first to admit that they are not all perfect. Most of them are a mixture of quiet saint and noisy sinner, like the rest of us. However, living with the re-enactment of the death of Jesus as the centre of Village life seems to have an effect, and each of them is probably just a little better than they would be if they lived somewhere else. It shows in the courtesy and kindness with which they treat the crowds of visitors who disrupt the life of their Village when they come to see the Play.

The Crucifixion according to Matthew 27:33–66

And when they came to a place called Golgotha (which means Place of a Skull), they offered Jesus wine to drink, mixed with gall; but when he tasted it, he would not drink it. And when they had crucified him, they divided his clothes among themselves by casting lots; then they sat down there and kept watch over him. Over his head they put the charge against him, which read, 'This is Jesus, the King of the Jews.'

Then two bandits were crucified with him, one on his right and one on his left. Those who passed by derided him, shaking their heads and saying, 'You who would destroy the temple and build it in three days, save yourself! If you are the Son of God, come down from the cross.' In the same way the chief priests also, along with the scribes and elders, were mocking him, saying, 'He saved others; he cannot save himself. He is the King of Israel; let him come down from the cross now, and we will believe in him. He trusts in God; let God deliver him now, if he wants to; for he said, "I am God's Son."' The bandits who were crucified with him also taunted him in the same way.

From noon on, darkness came over the whole land until three in the afternoon. And about three o'clock Jesus cried with a loud voice, 'Eli, Eli, lema sabachthani?' that is, 'My God, my God, why have you forsaken me?' When some of the bystanders heard it, they said, 'This man is calling for Elijah.' At once one of them ran and got a sponge, filled it with sour wine, put it on a stick, and gave it to him to drink. But the others said, 'Wait, let us see whether Elijah will come to save him.' Then Jesus cried again with a loud voice and breathed his last. At that moment the curtain of the temple was torn in two, from top to bottom. The earth shook, and the rocks were split. The tombs also were opened, and many bodies of the saints who had fallen asleep were raised. After his resurrection they came out of the tombs and entered the holy city and appeared to many. Now when the centurion and those with him, who were keeping watch over Jesus, saw the earthquake and what took place, they were terrified and said, 'Truly this man was God's Son!'

Many women were also there, looking on from a distance; they had followed Jesus from Galilee and had provided for him. Among them were Mary Magdalene, and Mary the mother of James and Joseph, and the mother of the sons of Zebedee.

When it was evening, there came a rich man from Arimathea, named Joseph, who was also a disciple of Jesus. He went to Pilate and asked for the body of Jesus; then Pilate ordered it to be given to him. So Joseph took the body and wrapped it in a clean linen cloth and laid it in his own new tomb, which he had hewn in the rock. He then rolled a great stone to the door of the tomb and went away. Mary Magdalene and the other Mary were there, sitting opposite the tomb.

The next day, that is, after the day of Preparation, the chief priests and the Pharisees gathered before Pilate and said, 'Sir, we remember what that impostor said while he was still alive, "After three days I will rise again." Therefore command the tomb to be made secure until the third day; otherwise his disciples may go and steal him away, and tell the people, "He has been raised from the dead," and the last deception would be worse than the first.' Pilate said to them, 'You have a guard of soldiers; go, make it as secure as you can.' So they went with the guard and made the tomb secure by sealing the stone. (NRSV)

Prayer

Lord, in your pierced hands we lay our heart;
Lord, at your pierced feet we choose our part;
Lord, in your wounded side
let us abide;
Amen.

Source unknown

Practical details

In this section we will cover the things which every pilgrim needs to know when they attend the Passion Play. (See also 'Useful Information' on p. vi above.)

Tickets

The Passion Play Theatre in Oberammergau was rebuilt in 1900, and has been enlarged since then to seat over 4,600 people. The seats are all numbered, and each ticket shows the door through which to enter.

Seating

Recent renovations provide more comfortable seats, under cover, with under-floor heating; but, even so, it is wise to bring (or to hire from the shops near the Theatre) a pillow or cushion to ease sitting still for five and a half hours.

Performances

In the year 2000 the Play will be performed five times a week, from 9 a.m. to about 11.30 a.m.; then, after a three-hour lunch break, the second part will last from 2.30 until 5.30 p.m.

Toilets

There are toilets near the entrance doors, accessible from the outside though you may re-enter on showing your ticket, and near the stage, accessible from inside the Theatre.

Jesus washes the disciples' feet.

Clothing

The audience is under cover but the stage is not. Some people say that the weather changes four times each day in Oberammergau. So it is advisable to wear layers of clothing which can be put on or taken off as it becomes colder or warmer. It can be very cold, so the shops near the Theatre also hire out blankets to wrap round you if required. It may rain on the way to the Theatre, so if you take a pair of slippers you can avoid having to sit in wet shoes.

Open air stage

The stage is in the open air. This does not mean that you can sneak a view of the action if you have no ticket: there are walls at the sides. The backdrop is formed by a ridge of mountains, with the constantly changing patterns of sun and clouds. Sometimes it happens that there is a thunderstorm at the time of the crucifixion. No artificial lighting is needed; with God as lighting manager, what drama could fail?

Rain

The cast and the front few rows of the audience will get wet if it rains, but there is a row of hair-driers and a change of costumes backstage if this happens, and the choir can wear raincoats under their robes. A cover is pulled over the orchestra, which is in a pit below the front of the stage, because it is impossible to play a wet violin.

The only time a performance was stopped by the weather was once when the stage was covered in hailstones.

English translation

Most visitors, unless they speak fluent German, will need to have an English translation of the Play. These will be provided with their ticket to those who have accommodation in the village only. Others will find them on sale in many hotels, in shops which display the sign *Textbuch*, and inside and outside the Theatre. While nobody would want to miss any of the action while their head is buried in a book, there is usually time during the sung choruses to read what is going to happen next. Even those who are entirely familiar with the events of the Gospels may need the text to see what connections are being made with the Old Testament scenes.

Lunch Breaks

Those who have overnight accommodation in the village will be given lunch tickets for selected restaurants serving only environmentally friendly food. There are many good restaurants, or you may buy sandwiches to eat in the open air.

Cameras

The villagers see the Passion Play as an act of worship. Therefore they want no applause, and cameras and camcorders are not allowed in the Theatre. Not only is it totally ineffective to use a flash-camera in a building of that size, but it is grossly discourteous to one's neighbours – who may be praying or in tears – to give the Play the atmosphere of a spectacle or a press conference. Visitors can buy excellent transparencies of the current year's Play, or postcards, or a picture book to show friends at home. These are far better than any pictures which an amateur photographer could take. There are also cassettes and compact disks of the music.

Videos

There is a video promoting tourism to the Village, but there will be no video of the Play itself. The villagers, rightly or wrongly, reply that they do not want their act of worship to be reproduced in people's living rooms. Groups of Satanists are also said to visit the Village, who might do unspeakable things with a video of the crucifixion.

Anybody who finds themselves sitting next to somebody who insists on using a camera during the Passion Play, or talking, or rustling sweet papers, will not help themselves or anybody else to gain more spiritual benefit from the Play by getting angry. The best advice is silently to pray for them.

Joab kisses his brother Amasa, then stabs him.

The Crucifixion according to Mark 15:22–47

Then they brought Jesus to the place called Golgotha (which means the place of a skull). And they offered him wine mixed with myrrh; but he did not take it. And they crucified him, and divided his clothes among them, casting lots to decide what each should take.

It was nine o'clock in the morning when they crucified him. The inscription of the charge against him read, 'The King of the Jews.' And with him they crucified two bandits, one on his right and one on his left. Those who passed by derided him, shaking their heads and saying, 'Aha! You who would destroy the temple and build it in three days, save yourself, and come down from the cross!' In the same way the chief priests, along with the scribes, were also mocking him among themselves and saying, 'He saved others; he cannot save himself. Let the Messiah, the King of Israel, come down from the cross now, so that we may see and believe.' Those who were crucified with him also taunted him.

When it was noon, darkness came over the whole land until three in the afternoon. At three o'clock Jesus cried out with a loud voice, 'Eloi, Eloi, lema sabachthani?' which means, 'My God, my God, why have you forsaken me?' When some of the bystanders heard it, they said, 'Listen, he is calling for Elijah.' And someone ran, filled a sponge with sour wine, put it on a stick, and gave it to him to drink, saying, 'Wait, let us see whether Elijah will come to take him down.' Then Jesus gave a loud cry and breathed his last. And the curtain of the temple was torn in two, from top to bottom. Now when the centurion, who stood facing him, saw that in this way he breathed his last, he said, 'Truly this man was God's Son!'

There were also women looking on from a distance; among them were Mary Magdalene, and Mary the mother of James the younger and of Joses, and Salome. These used to follow him and provided for him when he was in Galilee; and there were many other women who had come up with him to Jerusalem.

When evening had come, and since it was the day of Preparation, that is, the day before the sabbath, Joseph of Arimathea, a respected member of the council, who was also himself waiting expectantly for the kingdom of God, went boldly to Pilate and asked for the body of Jesus. Then Pilate wondered if he were already dead; and summoning the centurion, he asked him whether he had been dead for some time. When he learned from the centurion that he was dead, he granted the body to Joseph. Then Joseph bought a linen cloth, and taking down the body, wrapped it in the linen cloth, and laid it in a tomb that had been hewn out of the rock. He then rolled a stone against the door of the tomb. Mary Magdalene and Mary the mother of Joses saw where the body was laid. (NRSV)

Prayer

We give you thanks because for our salvation Jesus was obedient even to death on the cross. The tree of shame was made the tree of glory; and where life was lost, there life has been restored.

Adapted from *The Roman Missal*

'The Play's the Thing'

What can you expect to see when you attend the Passion Play?

Changes in the text

The Villagers of Oberammergau voted to continue using the text of the Passion Play that was written in 1870 by Joseph Alois Daisenberger, replacing an even older text. But each time the Play is performed, small changes are introduced to that text, and lines or scenes missed out, to bring it more in tune with modern thinking.

The Director of the production in 1990 and again in 2000 is Christian Stückl, and the Second Director is Otto Huber, who feels passionately about the text of the Passion, and together they have produced a revision. They have been advised by Ludwig Mödl, professor of Pastoral Theology at the University of Munich, and appointed by both the Lutheran Bishop of Bavaria and the Roman Catholic Bishop of Upper Bavaria.

They have made Jesus an even stronger figure than before, and have also brought out the strength of personality in the Virgin Mary and Mary Magdalene. Some new *tableaux vivants* have been added, showing Moses as a saviour of his people, foreshadowing Jesus. They have brought back, with new words, some of the music of Rochus Dedler, which had been omitted when more obscure scenes were dropped in previous years.

Antisemitism

Although few Germans alive in 2000 were old enough at the time of the holocaust to influence events, they are very conscious that false interpretations of some passages in the Gospels led to antisemitism. Such passages have been left out of successive revisions of the text in Oberammergau and the scenery and costumes, which will be very colourful in 2000, emphasise that Jesus and his followers were all of the Jewish race. Judas Iscariot is no longer shown as mad or evil but as a human being who made disastrously wrong choices. Jesus' teaching in the Sermon on the Mount, although it occurred earlier in Galilee, is likely to have been repeated by him on numerous occasions, and is shown as the reason for his condemnation. Subtle changes are also made in the presentation of the Jewish leaders, King Herod and Pontius Pilate.

No excuse can be made for antisemitism in the past, but the Villagers hope the Passion

Play will discourage it in future. Whatever our race, they say, we are all Israel, all guilty of the type of sin which caused the death of Jesus, and all equally blessed by his love.

Scenes from the Scriptures

The Play begins with verses spoken by the Prologue. Then the large choir sings a meditation on the events we are about to see, and how they are the fulfilment of the promises made in the Jewish Scriptures.

Then the choir divides and the curtains at the back of the stage open to reveal a *tableau vivant* of a scene from the Scriptures. These stationary scenes, which used to be quite common on the stage, are seldom seen anywhere else these days. It is a marvel how still the actors, including young children, can hold their pose for a minute or so until the curtains close again.

Typology

The *tableaux* rely on the system known as 'typology', which finds events in the Hebrew Scriptures which resemble events in the New Testament. The resemblances are often allegorical, and sometimes quite obscure, but at the time the Play was written this was the normal way of interpreting the Old Testament.

The Apocrypha

One of the *tableaux* is taken from the Book of Tobit. When Saint Paul wrote that 'all Scriptures are inspired by God' (2 Timothy 3:16), he was probably thinking of the Greek Bible, which includes Tobit and several other books not found in the Hebrew version. They are therefore included in the Old Testament section of Roman Catholic Bibles. Lutherans, Anglicans, and some other Protestants, however, call them the 'Apocrypha' (meaning 'hidden') and insert them between the Old and New Testaments.

Palm Sunday

Then the choir leave the stage and a scene from the Gospels begins. The Play opens with the events of Palm Sunday, and there is always a gasp of delight from the audience when the actor portraying Jesus enters, riding on a donkey which seems hardly big enough to carry him. Around 600 people are on stage to wave palm branches and welcome him.

The fickleness of crowds

Later in the Play the same crowd is easily whipped up by the leaders into shouting for the death of Jesus: 'Crucify him, crucify him!' The stage is so close to the audience that spectators feel almost as though they were part of that crowd. When we see how easily any crowd can be persuaded to do evil things by mass hysteria, we realise that we are all as much in need of the forgiveness that God offers as those who killed the Son of God.

Jesus in the Temple

When Jesus drives the traders from the Temple, it is impressive to see whole cages full of doves released and flying high into the sky above the Passion Theatre. But, of course, they will then fly off to a dovecote somewhere, to be collected and returned to the Theatre for the next day's performance!

The Crucifixion according to Luke 23:33–56

When they came to the place that is called The Skull, they crucified Jesus there with the criminals, one on his right and one on his left. Then Jesus said, 'Father, forgive them; for they do not know what they are doing.' And they cast lots to divide his clothing. And the people stood by, watching; but the leaders scoffed at him, saying, 'He saved others; let him save himself if he is the Messiah of God, his chosen one!' The soldiers also mocked him, coming up and offering him sour wine, and saying, 'If you are the King of the Jews, save yourself!' There was also an inscription over him, 'This is the King of the Jews.' One of the criminals who were hanged there kept deriding him and saying, 'Are you not the Messiah? Save yourself and us!' But the other rebuked him, saying, 'Do you not fear God, since you are under the same sentence of condemnation? And we indeed have been condemned justly, for we are getting what we deserve for our deeds, but this man has done nothing wrong.' Then he said, 'Jesus, remember me when you come into your kingdom.' He replied, 'Truly I tell you, today you will be with me in Paradise.'

It was now about noon, and darkness came over the whole land until three in the afternoon, while the sun's light failed; and the curtain of the temple was torn in two. Then Jesus, crying with a loud voice, said, 'Father, into your hands I commend my spirit.' Having said this, he breathed his last. When the centurion saw what had taken place, he praised God and said, 'Certainly this man was innocent.' And when all the crowds who had gathered there for this spectacle saw what had taken place, they returned home, beating their breasts. But all his acquaintances, including the women who had followed him from Galilee, stood at a distance, watching these things.

Now there was a good and righteous man named Joseph, who, though a member of the council, had not agreed to their plan and action. He came from the Jewish town of Arimathea, and he was waiting expectantly for the kingdom of God. This man went to Pilate and asked for the body of Jesus. Then he took it down, wrapped it in a linen cloth, and laid it in a rock-hewn tomb where no one had ever been laid. It was the day of Preparation, and the sabbath was beginning. The women who had come with him from Galilee followed, and they saw the tomb and how his body was laid. Then they returned, and prepared spices and ointments. On the sabbath they rested according to the commandment. (NRSV)

Crucifixion Prayers

Father, you have made us all in your likeness and you love all whom you have made; suffer not our family to separate itself from you by building barriers of race or colour. As your Son our Saviour was born of a Hebrew mother, but rejoiced in the faith of a Syrian woman and of a Roman soldier, welcomed the Greeks who sought him, and suffered a man from Africa to carry his cross; so teach us to regard the members of all races as fellow heirs of the kingdom of Jesus Christ our Lord. Amen.

By courtesy of Toc H and Oliver Warner

God of all the world, Jesus of Nazareth was born a Jew; so have mercy, we pray, on your ancient people, that they may continue to grow in the love of your name and in faithfulness to your covenant. Fetch us all home to your fold, so that we become one flock under the shepherd of Israel. Amen.

Adapted from *A New Zealand Prayer Book*

We believe that God,
who made the world and everything in it,
is Lord of heaven and earth.
God is too great to be contained
by any human construct.
God gives life and breath to everyone.
He has made all races to be brothers and sisters,
so that we should look for God,
and find the One whom we are seeking.
Yet God is not far from each one of us:
in God we live and move,
and all of us are God's children.
This we believe,
and this we proclaim! Amen.

Michael Counsell
in *More Prayers for Sundays* (from Acts 17:24–28)

Mutual absolution
I ask your forgiveness for what my people and I have done to you and yours, and I forgive you for what your ancestors did to my ancestors. Will you do the same for me?

We ask your forgiveness for what our people and we have done to you and yours, and we forgive you for what your ancestors did to our ancestors.

Now God has forgiven our sins, and torn the heavy veil of guilt, suspicion and bitterness which divided us. We are all children of God; we are sisters and brothers in God's family of love.

Amen.

Michael Counsell
in *More Prayers for Sundays*

Doves fly away at the cleansing of the temple.

An Outline of the Play in 2000

Morning

PRELUDE: The life which Adam lost at the tree of Paradise is won back by Christ at the tree of the Cross.

Tableau vivant: Adam is banished from Paradise *(Genesis 3)*, and the Cross is honoured.

Prologue. Chorus: 'God Eternal, hear your children.'

I. Entry into Jerusalem.
1. Jesus enters Jerusalem on a donkey.
2. He drives the traders from the Temple.
3. The question about authority, the most important commandment, Parable of the vineyard.
4. Reaction of the priests.

II. The meal in Bethany, and Jesus' farewell to his Mother.

Tableau vivant: Tobias says farewell to his parents *(Tobit 5, Apocrypha)*, and leaves to bring salvation.

Tableau vivant: The Bride in the Song of Solomon looks for her bridegroom. *(Song of Songs 3, 6)*

1. Jesus sends out the Twelve disciples and commands them to bear fearless witness.
2. Jesus is received by his friends at Bethany, and anointed by Mary Magdalene. He predicts his suffering and death.
3. Jesus' concern for Judas.
4. Jesus says farewell to his mother Mary.
5. Judas struggles with his doubts.

III. Jesus denounces the Teachers of the Law — Preparation for the Arrest.

Tableau vivant: Moses, carrying the tablets with the commandments, finds the people worshipping a golden calf. *(Exodus 32)*

1. The Sermon on the Mount.
2. The priests try to win over the people.
3. Jesus denounces the Teachers of the Law and the Pharisees.
4. The priests prepare to arrest Jesus.
5. Judas is ready to hand Jesus over.

6. For the life of Jesus, the purchase price of a slave is agreed on.
7. The Supreme Council agrees on the death of Jesus, though some members disagree with the decision.

IV. The Last Supper.

Tableau vivant: The Passover meal of the Israelites during the exodus from Egypt. *(Exodus 12)*

1. Jesus washes his disciples' feet and shares the meal of the Passover Lamb with them.
2. Jesus' words of farewell.

V. On the Mount of Olives.

Tableau vivant: Moses meets God in a burning bush. *(Exodus 3)*
Tableau vivant: Joseph is sold by his brothers *(Genesis 37)*

1. Judas leads the temple guard to Gethsemane.
2. Jesus comforts his disciples and prays for them.
3. Jesus prays in agony, and is strengthened by an angel.
4. Judas betrays Jesus with a kiss. Jesus is arrested.

Chorus: 'Pain's grievous battle is beginning.'

Afternoon

VI. Jesus is examined and mistreated by Annas — Peter denies that he knows Jesus, and his remorse.

Tableau vivant: Naboth is condemned by false witnesses. *(1 Kings 21)*
Tableau vivant: Daniel is unjustly condemned to be thrown into a den of lions. *(Daniel 6)*
Tableau vivant: Job is ridiculed because of his faith. *(Job 2)*

1. Annas the High Priest waits for Jesus, who is in prison.
2. Judas learns that Jesus is going to die.
3. Jesus is interrogated and struck.
4. Peter, when ridiculed, denies knowing his Master.
5. The temple guard accuse Jesus of being a false prophet and pretending to be a king.
6. Jesus is led before Caiaphas, the other High Priest .
7. Peter repents his denial and hopes for mercy.

VII. Judas' agony of conscience. Jesus is sentenced to death by the Supreme Council. Judas despairs.

Tableau vivant: Cain is conscience stricken for killing his brother. *(Genesis 4)*

1. Judas suffers agonies of conscience.
2. The Supreme Council prepares for the proceedings against Jesus.

3. Jesus is accused by false witnesses and condemned to death by the Council.
4. Judas bewails his betrayal of Jesus.
5. Judas despairs and ends his life.

VIII. Jesus before the Roman Governor Pontius Pilate and King Herod.

Tableau vivant: Moses before the Egyptian Pharaoh. *(Exodus 5)*
1. Jesus is bound and handed over to Pilate.
2. The leaders of the Council assemble before Pilate.
3. The Council demand that Pilate should condemn Jesus to death.
4. Pilate interrogates Jesus and asks about his Kingdom.
5. Pilate's wife is frightened by a dream about Jesus.
6. Pilate consults his staff.
7. Pilate abdicates his responsibility and refers the fate of Jesus to Herod.
8. Herod interrogates Jesus and mocks him.
9. Jesus is led before Pilate again.
10. Caiaphas attempts to stir up the crowd.
11. Jesus is whipped and crowned with thorns as a mock-king.
Tenor solo and Choir: 'Behold the king . . . behold the man.'

IX. Jesus is condemned to death on the cross.

Tableau vivant: In contrast to Jesus, Joseph is acclaimed by the people as their saviour. *(Genesis 41)*
1. Stirred up by the priests, the crowd reject Jesus.
2. Pilate releases Barabbas and condemns Jesus to death on the cross.

X. The Way of the Cross to the place of execution on the hill of Golgotha — the suffering and death of Jesus on the cross.

Tableau vivant: Abraham is ready to offer his son Isaac as a sacrifice, and the son carries the wood for the sacrifice himself to Mount Moriah. *(Genesis 22)*

Tableau vivant: Looking at the bronze snake which Moses lifts up, brings healing and salvation when in danger of death. *(Numbers 21, John 3.14)*
1. Mary follows her son on the way of the cross.
2. Carrying his cross, Jesus is led out to Golgotha.
3. Mary meets her son.
4. Simon of Cyrene helps Jesus to carry the cross.
5. Jesus meets the women of Jerusalem. Veronica wipes his face with a cloth.
Prologue: 'Up, good people . . .'

6. Jesus is lifted up on the cross and mocked.
7. The last words of Jesus and his death.
8. The soldier's spear pierces Jesus' heart.
9. Joseph of Arimathea requests permission to bury the body. The High Priests demand a guard to keep watch over it.
10. Jesus is taken down from the cross and laid in his Mother's arms.

Song at the Tomb.

XI. 'On the third day he rose again in accordance with the Scriptures; he ascended into heaven and is seated at the right hand of the Father!'
1. Christ rises from the tomb.
2. The angel shows the women the empty tomb.
3. Christ appears to Mary Magdalene.

Epilogue: He is risen! Rejoice, all who dwell in heaven!
Final tableau: Halleluiah! Praise the one who conquers sin and death!

The Crucifixion Scene at the Passion Play.

The Crucifixion according to John 19:17–42

So they took Jesus; and carrying the cross by himself, he went out to what is called The Place of the Skull, which in Hebrew is called Golgotha. There they crucified him, and with him two others, one on either side, with Jesus between them. Pilate also had an inscription written and put on the cross. It read, 'Jesus of Nazareth, the King of the Jews.' Many of the Jews read this inscription, because the place where Jesus was crucified was near the city; and it was written in Hebrew, in Latin, and in Greek. Then the chief priests of the Jews said to Pilate, 'Do not write, "The King of the Jews," but, "This man said, I am King of the Jews."' Pilate answered, 'What I have written I have written.' When the soldiers had crucified Jesus, they took his clothes and divided them into four parts, one for each soldier. They also took his tunic; now the tunic was seamless, woven in one piece from the top. So they said to one another, 'Let us not tear it, but cast lots for it to see who will get it.' This was to fulfill what the scripture says, 'They divided my clothes among themselves, and for my clothing they cast lots.' And that is what the soldiers did.

Meanwhile, standing near the cross of Jesus were his mother, and his mother's sister, Mary the wife of Clopas, and Mary Magdalene. When Jesus saw his mother and the disciple whom he loved standing beside her, he said to his mother, 'Woman, here is your son.' Then he said to the disciple, 'Here is your mother.' And from that hour the disciple took her into his own home.

After this, when Jesus knew that all was now finished, he said (in order to fulfill the scripture), 'I am thirsty.' A jar full of sour wine was standing there. So they put a sponge full of the wine on a branch of hyssop and held it to his mouth. When Jesus had received the wine, he said, 'It is finished.' Then he bowed his head and gave up his spirit.

Since it was the day of Preparation, the Jews did not want the bodies left on the cross during the sabbath, especially because that sabbath was a day of great solemnity. So they asked Pilate to have the legs of the crucified men broken and the bodies removed. Then the soldiers came and broke the legs of the first and of the other who had been crucified with him. But when they came to Jesus and saw that he was already dead, they did not break his legs. Instead, one of the soldiers pierced his side with a spear, and at once blood and water came out. (He who saw this has testified so that you also may believe. His testimony is true, and he knows that he tells the truth.) These things occurred so that the scripture might be fulfilled, 'None of his bones shall be broken.' And again another passage of scripture says, 'They will look on the one whom they have pierced.'

After these things, Joseph of Arimathea, who was a disciple of Jesus, though a secret one because of his fear of the Jews, asked Pilate to let him take away the body of Jesus. Pilate gave him permission; so he came and removed his body. Nicodemus, who had at first come to Jesus by night, also came, bringing a mixture of myrrh and aloes, weighing about a hundred pounds. They took the body of Jesus and wrapped it with the spices in linen cloths, according to the burial custom of the Jews. Now there was a garden in the place where he was crucified, and in the garden there was a new tomb in which no one had ever been laid. And so, because it was the Jewish day of Preparation, and the tomb was nearby, they laid Jesus there.
(NRSV)

Prayers

Blessed be your name, O Jesu, Son of the most high God;
blessed be the sorrow you suffered when your holy hands and
feet were nailed to the tree; and blessed your love when, the
fulness of pain accomplished, you gave your soul into the
hands of the Father; so by your cross and precious blood
redeeming all the world, all longing souls departed and the
numberless unborn; for now you are alive and reign, in the
glory of the eternal Trinity, God for ever and ever. Amen.

Adapted from Jeremy Taylor (1613–67)

We thank you that at your mystical supper, Son of God, you
receive us as partakers; we will not speak of the mystery to
your enemies; we will not let our lips touch your body with a
Judas-kiss; but like the thief we will acknowledge you:
Remember us when you come in your kingdom, O Jesus Christ
our Lord. Amen.

Adapted from *The Liturgy
of St John Chrysostom*

Evangelicals and Evangelists

Although some Christians call themselves 'Evangelicals' and others do not, all may be equally moved by the Passion Play. The word 'Evangelical' simply means 'true to the spirit of the Gospels'.

Historical accuracy

How historical is the Passion Play? Apart from the tradition about Veronica wiping the face of Jesus on his way to Golgotha, everything which is portrayed in the Play is taken from the Old Testament, the Apocrypha and the Gospels of Matthew, Mark, Luke and John. Many scholars seem to be returning to the view that at least one and maybe all four of these accounts of what Jesus said and did could have been written before, or soon after, Jerusalem was destroyed by the Romans in AD 70, about forty years after the resurrection of Jesus.

Anyone who is more than forty years old will agree that forty years is a very short time! If anyone now tried to pass off as true an inaccurate account of what happened forty years ago, there would be any number of eye-witnesses around to correct them.

So, although some of the sayings from earlier in the life of Jesus have been transposed to Holy Week for dramatic effect in the Passion Play, and allowing for a tendency to make the Last Supper, for instance, look more like an Old Master painting than the reality actually did, we may say that what appears on the stage in Oberammergau is very nearly what happened in Jerusalem about 2,000 years ago. In fact some have said that attending the Passion Play is second only to a pilgrimage to the Holy Land as a way of meeting the real Jesus face to face.

The actors

Anyone who wishes to act, sing or play in the Passion Play must have been born in Oberammergau or have lived there for at least five years. All the major parts are now each performed by two actors taking turns in alternate performances. They are all elected by a committee.

Previously any woman appearing on stage had to be unmarried, so some concern was expressed by the more conservative villagers at the departure from tradition when one of the women chosen to take the part of the Virgin Mary in 1990 was a married woman with children. Most people agree, however, that this is less illogical than having the role of the mother performed by a woman who is several years younger than the man taking the part of her son. It was even rumoured that previously some women were having children but postponing their marriage in order to have a chance of being chosen for a part in the Play under the old rules.

Good news

The word we translate as 'gospel' is, in the original Greek of the New Testament, ευαγγελιον, meaning 'good news'. 'Evangelical', then, means 'concerning the gospel', so surely we ought never to use the word in a way that excludes some people or groups, since the gospel excludes nobody.

The Passion Play truly portrays what is described in the four Gospels, and therefore it is definitely Evangelical.

Evangelism

Evangelism is the process of sharing the good news with other people. When somebody has heard and understood the good news that God loves them, it would be selfish to keep it to themselves. In this sense, every Christian must be an evangelist, and what happens at Oberammergau is evangelistic, because many people, who have heard about the crucifixion of Jesus, realise there for the first time what it means for each of them as an individual.

Emotions

It would be wrong to stir up false emotionalism, which has no lasting effects. For most people, however, to realise how much they are loved is a very

---

The death and resurrection of Jesus

+ reveals the love of God and God's understanding of our suffering;
+ sets an example of heroic courage and compassion for us to follow;
+ overcomes the power of guilt;
+ provides a sacrifice which, when we identify with it by faith, brings the forgiveness of our sins;
+ conquers the power of sin and death and leads us to eternal life;
+ brings about reconciliation or 'at-one-ment' between us and God.

Who would not be grateful to God when they realise that this is what Jesus has done?

emotional experience. Stiff-upper-lipped English gentlemen can sometimes be seen at the Passion Play struggling to resist the tears which other people are shedding unashamedly. But true emotion is what moves people to good behaviour. Good evangelism is bound to be emotional, without being falsely so.

---

2 Corinthians 5:14–20

For the love of Christ urges us on, because we are convinced that one has died for all; therefore all have died. And he died for all, so that those who live might live no longer for themselves, but for him who died and was raised for them. From now on, therefore, we regard no one from a human point of view; even though we once knew Christ from a human point of view, we know him no longer in that way. So if anyone is in Christ, there is a new creation: everything old has passed away; see, everything has become new! All this is from God, who reconciled us to himself through Christ, and has given us the ministry of reconciliation; that is, in Christ God was reconciling the world to himself, not counting their trespasses against them, and entrusting the message of reconciliation to us. So we are ambassadors for Christ, since God is making his appeal through us; we entreat you on behalf of Christ, be reconciled to God. (NRSV)

Prayer

Lord Jesus Christ, you stretched out your arms of love on the hard wood of the cross that everyone might come within the reach of your saving embrace: so clothe us in your Spirit that we, reaching forth our hands in love, may bring those who do not know you to the knowledge and love of you; for the honour of your name. Amen.

US Book of Common Prayer 1979
from Charles Henry Brent (1862–1929)

Reactions

When they come out of the Passion Play Theatre, how do people react to what they have seen?

Tears and anger

I met some who had wept at the story of the unjust death of a good man, but who did not believe that Jesus was anything more than that. Jesus himself said, 'Weep not for me but for yourselves.'

When people say they have no faith, they often mean that the picture of God which they have been given is not big enough to meet their problems. They need a larger idea of God.

It makes poor sense to blame God for all the suffering in the world, and at the same time to allege that there is no God. Jesus wanted us to see that his own self-sacrificing love for us is a reflection of the way God loves us.

The cross of Christ

Many people have looked at the cross of Christ and have realized that God shares all our pain and grief; it is a sort of 'cross-section' of the pain in the heart of God.

The Resurrection of Jesus.

It is not that unbelievers have no god; it would be more true to say that their ideas about God are not yet developed enough – they are 'between gods'.

Others whom I met in Oberammergau believed that there is a God, or that there might possibly be one, but were having to re-think their attitude to life.

Talking to God

Jesus taught his followers to talk to God as naturally as children talk to their parents. Many visitors want to pray when they have seen the Passion Play. Simply talking to God in your own words is best, but this book contains some suggestions for those who find that difficult.

A little girl was once told to 'Think before you speak.' She replied, 'How can I know what I think until I've heard what I say?' Talking to others helps us to sort out our own ideas. The staff of the Oberammergau English Language Church Welcome Centre often find that people want to talk with them after the Play. Sharing reactions to the Play with others on the journey home can also be useful.

Telling others

It would be selfish to keep to ourselves any new insights into Jesus and God which we have found on our journey. So visitors usually want to tell their friends and neighbours about the Play when they reach home.

Deeper commitment

Many people react to the Play with a deeper commitment to God, or even by putting God in charge of their lives for the first time. They have seen what Jesus has done for them. In gratitude, they want to promise to pray more, and to love God and their neighbour more deeply. Telling somebody else about this decision is a way of showing that there will be no going back.

God understands

Shortly before my wife and I were booked to see the 1984 Passion Play, our five-year-old son Simon was knocked down and killed by a drunk driver. Our other children insisted that we should still go to Oberammergau, but I was very angry with God. Then I saw the actress playing the part of the Virgin Mary looking at the dead body of her son Jesus, killed, as far as she could see, unjustly and pointlessly. I felt that Mary understood what I was going through.

Then I remembered that Jesus is not only Mary's son but God's Son also. In a sense, God too was looking at the dead body of his own Son. Yet God was able to bring good out of the tragedy. It sounds absurd, but at that moment it was as if I forgave God for the death of Simon.

I knew that God too understood what I was feeling. So I needed God to forgive my anger against him. I felt as though I had been one of the angry crowd who had caused the death of Jesus. Yet how was I to say the Lord's Prayer if I did not forgive others as God had forgiven me? So after talking it over, my wife and I wrote a letter to the driver who had caused our son's death, telling him we had forgiven him. It was the only reaction we could think of that was appropriate to what we had seen at Oberammergau.

John 12:23–25

Jesus said, 'The hour has come for the Son of Man to be glorified. Very truly, I tell you, unless a grain of wheat falls into the earth and dies, it remains just a single grain; but if it dies, it bears much fruit. Those who love their life lose it, and those who hate their life in this world will keep it for eternal life.' (NRSV)

Prayer

Most merciful God, who by the death and resurrection of your Son Jesus Christ delivered and saved us all: grant that by faith in him who suffered on the cross, we may triumph in the power of his victory; through Jesus Christ our Lord. Amen.

Scottish Book of Common Prayer 1912

Oberammergau Parish Church

Another response to the Play is a desire to worship God with other Christians.

Daily Mass

There is a daily Mass in the Roman Catholic Parish Church of Oberammergau. The Mass is sometimes in German, sometimes in English or partly in each language, and visiting priests are invited to concelebrate.

The onion-shaped dome of the Parish Church rises over the Village. The church was built in 1749 on the site of the church where the vow had been made. It was decorated by local artists in a blend of Baroque and Rococo styles.

The high altar

The theme of the high altar is the Rosary: St Dominic receives the string of Rosary beads from the Virgin Mary, while St Catherine of Siena receives the crown of thorns from Jesus Christ.

Pieta: the Virgin Mary cradles her dead son.

The sanctuary

The statues in the sanctuary from left to right are: St Joseph with the child Jesus; St Peter with the cross on which he was crucified upside down, with the keys of the kingdom and a cock whose crowing marked Peter's betrayal; St Paul with the sword of the Spirit; St Joachim with doves.

The paintings on the walls of the sanctuary are, on the left, Jesus teaching the Lord's Prayer, and, on the right, the angel announcing to Mary that she will bear a son. The medallions in the sanctuary are the symbols of the four Gospels: an angel for St Matthew; an eagle for St John; a lion for St Mark and an ox for St Luke.

The side altars

The side altars nearest the sanctuary are, on the left, the altar of the Holy Trinity, with statues of St Martin and St Gregory, and a painting, at the top, of the beheading of St Barbara; while on the right is the altar of the Holy Cross. The crucifix, from the previous gothic church, is the one in front of which the Village elders made their vow in 1633. The statues on this altar represent Dismas the good thief, Mary, John and Mary Magdalene, and the painting at the top is of the beheading of St Catherine of Alexandria.

Next to the altar of the Holy Cross is a pieta depicting Mary cradling the body of her dead son, which is also from the gothic church.

The side altars in the middle are, on the left, the altar of St Anne, the Virgin Mary's mother, with a painting and an old statue of Anne, Mary and Jesus, and statues of St Sebastian with a bow and St Rochus, both of whom were invoked against the plague; on the right, the altar of St Anthony of Padua, a Franciscan, with statues of St Clare and St Francis of Assisi, John the Baptist and St John Nepamuk.

The pulpit has a relief of Jesus the Good Shepherd.

The dome

Around the dome is a fresco showing Saints Peter and Paul, to whom the church is dedicated, saying farewell as they come out of the city of Rome to be martyred. Peter is crucified upside down (because he said he was not worthy to die in the same way as his Master) and Paul is beheaded with a sword. In the centre of the dome is the Holy Trinity – Father, Son and Holy Spirit – surrounded by figures from the Bible. The medallions under the fresco represent St Augustine of Hippo (burning heart); St Ambrose (bee-hive); St Gregory (musical notes) and St Jerome (books).

Above the organ loft there is a painting of the altar of St

Peter's in Rome. There are scenes from the Bible on the galleries with, in the centre under the organ, Moses lifting up the bronze serpent, which is one of the *tableaux* in the Passion Play.

Among the carvings in the church, that of Christ sitting on a donkey is on a pole used to lead the procession on Palm Sunday.

Passion Play Model

Under the tower at the back of the church is a beautiful new carved and painted wooden model of scenes from the passion. Drop a coin in the slot, and it will be illuminated to the accompaniment of music from the Play.

Choir and orchestra

Those who attend Sunday morning Mass in the Parish Church will find it led by the choir and orchestra who also perform at the Passion Play. They are all amateurs, but the word 'amateur' comes from the Latin *amor*, meaning 'love', and they all have an excellent standard. Somebody once remarked that Noah's ark was built by amateurs, but the *Titanic* was made by professionals!

The churchyard

The grave of Rochus Dedler, the Village schoolmaster who died in 1821 and wrote the Haydnesque music for the

Play, is outside the Parish Church facing the north door. The names on the graves in the churchyard show that the families who are involved in the Passion Play today have lived in the Village for generations.

Information

In the Play season Masses in German are on weekdays at 8 a.m. and 7.30 p.m., and on Sundays at 7 and 10 a.m. and 12 noon and 7.30 p.m. Mass in English in the Parish Church will be at 6 p.m. on the days the Play is performed. In other years Masses are on Sundays and Festivals at 9.30 a.m. and 11 a.m. and Tuesdays, Thursdays, Fridays and Saturdays at 7 p.m., and Wednesdays at 8 a.m. Confessions are heard before services.

Guided tours of the church in German and English during Play years are on Sundays, Mondays, Wednesdays, Fridays and Saturdays at 1.30 p.m.

There is organ music after the 7.30 p.m. Mass, and an introduction to the Passion Play in German at 8.15 p.m., on Sundays, Tuesdays, Thursdays and Saturdays in Play years.

Luke 24:1–12

On the first day of the week, at early dawn, they came to the tomb, taking the spices that they had prepared. They found the stone rolled away from the tomb, but when they went in, they did not find the body. While they were perplexed about this, suddenly two men in dazzling clothes stood beside them. The women were terrified and bowed their faces to the ground, but the men said to them, 'Why do you look for the living among the dead? He is not here, but has risen. Remember how he told you, while he was still in Galilee, that the Son of Man must be handed over to sinners, and be crucified, and on the third day rise again.' Then they remembered his words, and returning from the tomb, they told all this to the eleven and to all the rest. Now it was Mary Magdalene, Joanna, Mary the mother of James, and the other women with them who told this to the apostles. But these words seemed to them an idle tale, and they did not believe them. But Peter got up and ran to the tomb; stooping and looking in, he saw the linen cloths by themselves; then he went home, amazed at what had happened. (NRSV)

Prayer

O Lord Jesu Christ, Son of the living God, we pray you to set your passion, cross and death between your judgement and our souls, now and in the hour of our death. Vouchsafe to grant mercy and grace to the living, rest to the dead, to your holy Church peace and concord, and to us sinners everlasting life and glory; for you are alive and reign, with the Father and the Holy Spirit, one God for ever and ever. Amen.

Horae BVM
(pre-fourteenth century)

In the Lutheran Church and on the Way Home

The other church in Oberammergau is the Evangelical-Lutheran Church beside the Passion Play Theatre.

There are quite large numbers of German Protestants throughout Bavaria, and the Lutheran Pastor shares with the Catholic Priest in saying prayers with the cast of the Passion Play before each performance.

The Lutheran Church building is dedicated to the Cross, and they have a custom of inviting visitors to write their worries on slips of paper and to leave them pinned to a large wooden cross inside. Underneath the church is a hall where 'Open House' is held throughout the Play season.

Visitors' services

Because there are so many American Lutheran visitors, the Lutheran Church in Oberammergau brings in

The Crucifix before which the Vow was made.

additional bilingual pastors in Passion Play years, and they conduct their services in both English and German. It is a peaceful place for quiet meditation.

The ministers of the English-Language Church Welcome Centre will share in leading Holy Communion in the Lutheran Church immediately after the Play. Visiting ministers may request the use of the Roman Catholic hall for a service for the group they are leading.

Other churches

Some of those who have seen the Passion Play may have the opportunity to go into other churches on their way across Europe. It is a good custom to kneel to pray for the people who worship there, and to attend a service if possible, even if it is in a language you do not understand.

As the churches now grow closer together, one of the joys of travel is to discover how much we have in common with Christians of very different traditions, and what a warm welcome we receive from them when we identify ourselves as Christians. This fills us with a fresh desire to work and pray for mutual recognition and the restoration of visible unity between the churches.

Regular worship

One of the joyful responses we can make to the Passion Play when we return home is a resolve to be regular in worshipping in our own church. St Paul tells us that every time we break bread together we 'proclaim the Lord's death until he comes.' We can think of every Holy Communion, Eucharist or Mass as a Passion Play in which Jesus really comes to us, and we can make our own Vow, like that of the Oberammergau villagers, to receive him regularly at this 're-present-ation' of his death and resurrection.

Some people tell you it would be hypocritical to go to church unless you feel like it. If I only went to church when I felt like it I wouldn't get to church very often! Yet if Christians do go to church when their feelings are dry or even rebellious, and when the style of worship is not to their taste, that is an act of self-sacrifice which is pleasing to God, a 'sacrifice of praise'. It is amazing how often, by the end of the service, with this attitude, it has turned out to be enjoyable. The villagers of Oberammergau, with their faithfulness to their Vow, have something to teach us all.

Information

Services in the Lutheran Church (Theaterstraße 10, Oberammergau) are held in non-Play years on Sundays and Festivals at 10 a.m.

During the Play season, on all days when the Play is performed (Sunday, Monday,

Wednesday, Friday and Saturday) there is Ecumenical Morning Prayer at 8.15 a.m.; organ music at 8.30 a.m.; 'Open House' during the noon recess (information, an opportunity to talk to fellow visitors, and visit the reading room); organ music at 1.30 p.m.; Holy Communion (Anglican/Lutheran) in English, open to all Christians at 5.30 p.m.; Open House at 6 p.m.; organ music at 8.45 p.m. (8.15 in September); and Evening Prayer with Holy Communion at 8.30 p.m.

On non-Play days (Tuesdays and Thursdays) there is Open House at 6 p.m.; organ music at 8.15 p.m. Evening Prayer with Holy Communion at 9 p.m. (8.30 p.m. in September). Every Sunday there is Holy Communion at 10 a.m.

Luke 24:13–35

Now on that same day two of them were going to a village called Emmaus, about seven miles from Jerusalem, and talking with each other about all these things that had happened. While they were talking and discussing, Jesus himself came near and went with them, but their eyes were kept from recognizing him. And he said to them, 'What are you discussing with each other while you walk along?' They stood still, looking sad. Then one of them, whose name was Cleopas, answered him, 'Are you the only stranger in Jerusalem who does not know the things that have taken place there in these days?' He asked them, 'What things?'

They replied, 'The things about Jesus of Nazareth, who was a prophet mighty in deed and word before God and all the people, and how our chief priests and leaders handed him over to be condemned to death and crucified him. But we had hoped that he was the one to redeem Israel. Yes, and besides all this, it is now the third day since these things took place. Moreover, some women of our group astounded us. They were at the tomb early this morning, and when they did not find his body there, they came back and told us that they had indeed seen a vision of angels who said that he was alive. Some of those who were with us went to the tomb and found it just as the women had said; but they did not see him.'

Then he said to them, 'Oh, how foolish you are, and how slow of heart to believe all that the prophets have declared! Was it not necessary that the Messiah should suffer these things and then enter into his glory?' Then beginning with Moses and all the prophets, he interpreted to them the things about himself in all the scriptures.

As they came near the village to which they were going, he walked ahead as if he were going on. But they urged him strongly, saying, 'Stay with us, because it is almost evening and the day is now nearly over.' So he went in to stay with them. When he was at the table with them, he took bread, blessed and broke it, and gave it to them. Then their eyes were opened, and they recognized him; and he vanished from their sight.

They said to each other, 'Were not our hearts burning within us while he was talking to us on the road, while he was opening the scriptures to us?' That same hour they got up and returned to Jerusalem; and they found the eleven and their companions gathered together. They were saying, 'The Lord has risen indeed, and he has appeared to Simon!' Then they told what had happened on the road, and how he had been made known to them in the breaking of the bread. (NRSV)

Prayer

Almighty God, by the passion of your blessed Son you made an instrument of shameful death to be for us the means of life and peace: grant us so to glory in the cross of Christ, that we may gladly suffer for his sake; for he is alive and reigns with you and the Holy Spirit, one God, now and for ever. Amen.

Adapted from *The Prayer Book*
as proposed in 1928

The spies bring back grapes from the Promised Land.

Jesus Loves You

If I was asked to sum up in three words the message of the Passion Play and the reason for attending it, they would be 'God loves you.'

God knows you by name

The death and resurrection of Jesus tell of a completely personal love: God knows you by name, knows everything about you, and values you for what makes you different from any other person in the whole of creation. He accepts you as you are, though he will give you the power to change. God loves you.

It is not a case of human beings searching for a remote and uninterested God. God created the world so as to fill it with creatures that he could love. Some of those creatures, the human ones, he made capable of returning his love.

Then, when they misused their God-given freedom to love by rebelling against their Creator, God came to earth to search for them and to give his life in love for them.

A man named Jesus

The disciples did not realise this all at once. For three years they travelled the Holy Land with a man named Jesus who loved them and told them about treating God as if he were a loving Father. He said, 'Greater love has no one than this, to lay down one's life for one's friends.' (John 15:13)

Jesus could have avoided the cross, by telling lies in Gethsemane, leaving his disciples to suffer, or denying what he had taught them about a God who loves sinners. Instead he willingly sacrificed his life to save them. The disciples realised at last that the love they saw in Jesus revealed the self-sacrificing love of God.

An element of risk

There is an element of risk involved in making anything. It might not do what it is intended for; it might not work properly. All creative activity involves risk, and concentration on making it right. Bringing up children is also a creative activity. Parents give their children increasing freedom to make their own choices. This involves risk, and great pain when they go wrong.

14. Expulsion from Paradise

15. Jesus' entry into Jerusalem

16. Jesus teaching

7. Cleansing the Temple

8. The Last Supper

19. Judas betrays Jesus

20. Mockery by the soldiers

21. Interrogation by Herod

22. Jesus is whipped

23. Jesus is crowned with thorns

24. Sentenced by Pilate

25. Jesus dies on the cross

26. Final tableau

27. Jesus

28. Mary

This gives us an insight into the heart of God the Father. God took the risk of making human beings free, aware that we would not, at first, be loving and kind as he intended us to be. God planned to bring us to love him, by dying for us. The cross reveals the eternal pain in the heart of God as he struggles to create people who will respond to his love.

A leap of faith

On the Laber mountain above Oberammergau, the paragliders jump off the mountainside, trusting that the power of the invisible air will support them. We cannot see the love of God, though on the cross we can see its effects. Not until we have taken the leap of faith involved in giving God complete control of our lives can we know that God will support us and unstintingly give us his love through all eternity.

John 20

Early on the first day of the week, while it was still dark, Mary Magdalene came to the tomb and saw that the stone had been removed from the tomb. So she ran and went to Simon Peter and the other disciple, the one whom Jesus loved, and said to them, 'They have taken the Lord out of the tomb, and we do not know where they have laid him.' Then Peter and the other disciple set out and went toward the tomb. The two were running together, but the other disciple outran Peter and reached the tomb first. He bent down to look in and saw the linen wrappings lying there, but he did not go in. Then Simon Peter came, following him, and went into the tomb. He saw the linen wrappings lying there, and the cloth that had been on Jesus' head, not lying with the linen wrappings but rolled up in a place by itself. Then the other disciple, who reached the tomb first, also went in, and he saw and believed; for as yet they did not understand the scripture, that he must rise from the dead. Then the disciples returned to their homes.

But Mary stood weeping outside the tomb. As she wept, she bent over to look into the tomb; and she saw two angels in white, sitting where the body of Jesus had been lying, one at the head and the other at the feet. They said to her, 'Woman, why are you weeping?' She said to them, 'They have taken away my Lord, and I do not know where they have laid him.' When she had said this, she turned around and saw Jesus standing there, but she did not know that it was Jesus. Jesus said to her, 'Woman, why are you weeping? Whom are you look-ing for?' Supposing him to be the gardener, she said to him, 'Sir, if you have carried him away, tell me where you have laid him, and I will take him away.' Jesus said to her, 'Mary!' She turned and said to him in Hebrew, 'Rabbouni!' (which means Teacher). Jesus said to her, 'Do not hold on to me, because I have not yet ascended to the Father. But go to my brothers and say to them, "I am ascending to my Father and your Father, to my God and your God."' Mary Magdalene went and announced to the disciples, 'I have seen the Lord'; and she told them that he had said these things to her.

When it was evening on that day, the first day of the week, and the doors of the house where the disciples had met were locked for fear of the Jews, Jesus came and stood among them and said, 'Peace be with you.' After he said this, he showed them his hands and his side. Then the disciples rejoiced when they saw the Lord. Jesus said to them again, 'Peace be with you. As the Father has sent me, so I send you.' When he had said this, he breathed on them and said to them, 'Receive the Holy Spirit. If you forgive the sins of any, they are forgiven them; if you retain the sins of any, they are retained.' But Thomas (who was called the Twin), one of the twelve, was not with them when Jesus came. So the other disciples told him, 'We have seen the Lord.' But he said to them, 'Unless I see the mark of the nails in his hands, and put my finger in the mark of the nails and my hand in his side, I will not believe.'

A week later his disciples were again in the house, and Thomas was with them. Although the doors were shut, Jesus came and stood among them and said, 'Peace be with you.' Then he said to Thomas, 'Put your finger here and see my hands. Reach out your hand and put it in my side. Do not doubt but believe.' Thomas answered him, 'My Lord and my God!' Jesus said to him, 'Have you believed because you have seen me? Blessed are those who have not seen and yet have come to believe.'

Now Jesus did many other signs in the presence of his disciples, which are not written in this book. But these are written so that you may come to believe that Jesus is the Messiah, the Son of God, and that through believing you may have life in his name. (NRSV)

Prayer

Praise to you, Lord Jesus Christ, for all the benefits you have won for us, for all the pains and insults you have borne for us. Most merciful redeemer, friend and brother, may we know you more clearly, love you more dearly, and follow you more nearly, day by day. Amen.

St Richard of Chichester
(1197–1253)

Visiting Oberammergau in Other Years

It is not only in the years when the Passion Play is being performed that a visit to the Village can be rewarding. The villagers are keen that it should be a popular holiday centre at all times.

Walking, cycling and skiing

Oberammergau is an excellent centre for walking or cycling in summer and skiing in winter. A cable car carries visitors up the Laber Mountain to walk from the top. The chair-lift almost opposite the railway station takes one to the ridge along which a walk and a scramble lead to the cross on the top of the Koffel, the sugar-loaf shaped mountain which dominates Oberammergau.

Wall paintings

The walls of the houses, like many in the region, are decorated with paintings. Many are scenes from the Bible or the

Mary Magdalene sees the risen Christ.

lives of the saints, and paintings of the crucifixion remind us that in many ways, Oberammergau is a village under the cross. These wall paintings are referred to locally as *Lüftlmalerei*. The paint is applied while the plaster is still wet. The Village orphanage is covered with scenes from the story of Hansel and Gretel.

Local crafts

There is a good museum of local crafts near the centre of the main street. Then, in the Pilatushaus (so named because it has a wall painting of Jesus on trial before Pontius Pilate) there is often a local craftsman at work. The Pilatushaus is covered in staircases and balconies which are not real, but painted on the walls in *trompe l'oeil* (deceiving the eye) style. It is situated behind the Ammergauer Haus. See 'The Pilatushaus' under 'Useful Information' at the front of this book (p. xiii) for opening times and telephone numbers.

The villagers have for centuries made a living selling wood-carvings. In the Dorfstraße is a statue of one of the hawkers who used to leave the Village with frames on their backs covered in carvings. They used to travel as far as the Baltic and the Mediterranean, returning months later, after all their wares had been sold. Nowadays there is a school of wood-carving in Oberammergau.

Even in their first few years at school, the children of the Village are watched to see whether they have talents in art, music or drama, and are then groomed from an early age to take a part in the Play, the choir or the orchestra, or to train as a wood-carver.

The Passion Theatre

In the years when the Play is not being performed, visitors are taken backstage in the Passion Theatre to see the machinery for the scenery of the *tableaux*, and many rooms full of costumes, some of them very old and precious.

Oberammergau is becoming increasingly ecologically conscious, and in 1997 it was honoured with the national environmental prize.

Prayer

O Lord Jesus Christ, son of the living God, who at the evening hour didst rest in the sepulchre, and didst thereby sanctify the grave to be a bed of hope to thy people: Make us so to abound in sorrow for our sins, which were the cause of thy passion, that when our bodies lie in the dust, our souls may live with thee; who livest and reignest with the Father and the Holy Ghost, one God, world without end. Amen.

Compline, adapted from the *Sarum Breviary* by Edward Willis in the *Cuddesdon Office Book* 1880

Houses in Oberammergau.

Passion Plays in Other Places

Following are contact addresses in other places which are known to produce Passion Plays. Productions are every year unless otherwise indicated, in which case the years of the last production and the next production are given. When telephoning from the UK, dial 00, then the country code, then the full telephone number (omitting the first 0 where shown).

Last = last performed. Next = next performance.

EUROPASSION
A federation of groups in Europe which produce Passion Plays. Contact their Secretary General, Josef Lang, Europassion, Sitterswalde Straße 52-54, D-66271 Auersmacher, Germany. Tel: 06805 7589. Fax:200843.

AUSTRIA
(Country telephone code 43) Austrian National Tourist Office in London, 30 George Street, W1A 2QB. Tel: 0171 629 0461 Fax: 499 6038. E-mail oewlon@easynet.co.uk Internet http://austria.info.at/
Dorfstetten, 50 km. from Sankt Pölten, west of Vienna. Every 6 years, last 1996, next Jul. & Aug. in 2002. Enquiries Franz Puschenreitner, Wimbergeramt 67. Tickets Andreas Hochstöger, Forstamt 41A; A-4392 Dorfstetten, Austria. Tel: 07418 8354 Fax: 8255.
Erl, on the river Inn near Kufstein north of Innsbruck. Normally every six years; last 1997, next 2002, mid-May to end of Oct., Sat. & Sun. 12.30 to about 4.30 pm. Tourismusverband Erl, Dorf 15, A-6343 Erl (Tirol), Austria. Tel: 05373.8117 or 8139, Fax: 8487 or 8586. Internet http://www.tis.co.at/passion
Feldkirchen, near Graz. Every 3 years, last 1998, next 2001, Sat. & Sun. during Lent, 3-6 p.m. and Good Friday, 7 pm. Enquiries Claudia Potetz, Mühlweg 74, Tel: 0316 242662. During the play season Feldkirchner Passionspiele, Postfach 11, A-8073 Feldkirchen bei Graz, Austria. Tel & Fax: 0316 244343.
Kirchschlag in der buckligen Welt, 100 km. south of Vienna. Every 5 years, last 1995, next 2000, May - Oct. Sun. 1.30-5 p.m. Pfarramt, Passionspielstraße 3, A-2860 Kirchschlag, Austria. Tel: 02646 224314 Fax: 224310.
Mettmach, west of Salzburg. Last 1995, next 10 Jun.-23 Jul.

2000. Spielgemeinschaft Mettmach, A-4931 Mettmach (Ober-
Östereich), Austria. Tel & Fax: 07755 7155.
St Margarethen im Burgenland, 9 km from Eisenstadt, which
is 50 km. south of Vienna. Every 5 years, last 1996; next 2001, Jun.
to Sep., every Sun. & every other Sat., 4 p.m. - 7 p.m. Franz
Miehl, Passionspielbüro, Kirchengasse 20, A-7062, St
Margarethen, Austria. Tel: 02680 2100. Fax: 22344.
Thiersee, near Erl. Last 1994, next (200th anniversary) 1999, 5 Jun.
to 3 Oct., Sat. & Sun. 1-4.30 p.m. Passionspielverein, Voderthiersee
38, A-6335 Thiersee, Austria. Tel: 05376 5236. Fax: 5953.

BELGIUM
(Country telephone code 32) Belgian Tourist Office, 29 Princes
Street, London W1R 7RG. Tel (24 hour, premium charges): 0891
887799. Fax: 0171 629 0454.
Kelmis - La Calamine. Willy Debey, 36 Kirchplatz, B-4720
Kelmis, Belgium. Tel: 087 658778.
Ligny. Every Sun. in Lent 3.30 p.m. Confrérie de la Passion,
André Pesleut, 15 rue Gr& Cortil, B-5140 Ligny, Belgium.
Tel & Fax: 071 888476. Internet
http://www.club.innet.be/~year2488/public_html/passion1.htm
Mariekerke. Kultuurkring De Meivis, Raf Joos, Omgangstraat
126, B-2880 Mariekerke, Belgium. Tel: 052 330607. Fax: 331444.
Schönberg. Every 5 years; last Mar. 1998, Fri. & Sat. 8.30 p.m.,
Sun. 3 p.m. Marlene Backes, Atzerath 32, B- 4780 Sankt-Vith,
Belgium, Tel & Fax: 080 228521. During play season
Tel: 080 548444.
Sibret, South of Liège. Last 1995, next undecided. Cercle
Catholique Sibretois, c/o Alain Dubois, Chausée de Bastogne 92,
B-6640 Sibret, Belgium. Tel: 061 266466.

CANADA
(Country telephone code 1)
Montreal, Québec. Holy Cross Fathers, Oratoire Saint-Joseph,
3800 Chemin Queen Mary, Montréal, Québec, Canada. Metro
Cote-des-Neiges. Tel: (514) 733 8211.

CZECH REPUBLIC
(Country telephone code 420)
Horice na Sumave, Bohemia. Pasije Spolecnost pro Obvonu,
Pasijovyçh her, TS-382 22 Horice na Sumave, Czech Republic.
Tel: Miroslav Cunat 837 89101.

ENGLAND
(Country telephone code 44) British Tourist Authority, Thames
Tower, Black's Road, London W6 9EL. Tel: 0181 846 9000.
Fax: 0181 563 0302. Internet: www.visitbritain.com

Coventry, West Midlands. The Coventry mystery plays are performed in the ruins of the old Cathedral about every third year. Last 1997; next not known. Tourist Information Centre, Bayley Lane, Coventry CV1 5RN, England. Tel: 01203 832303. Fax: 832370. Coventry Cathedral Office, 7 Priory Row, Coventry CV1 5ES. Tel: 227597, Fax: 631448. The Belgrade Theatre box office. Tel: 553055.

Greenwich, South East London. Passion play planned for Good Friday 2000. Revd Dr Malcolm Torrey, 89 Westcombe Park Road, London SE3 7RZ, England. Tel: 0181 858 3006.

York, Yorkshire. The York Mystery Plays, usually every 4 years; Last 12 Jul. 1998; next in York Minster, mid-Jun. to mid-Jul. 2000. York Millennium Mystery Plays, POB 226, York YO3 6ZU, England. Tel: 01904 658338. Fax: 01904 612631. Box Office 01937 584123. E-mail yemf@netcomuk.co.uk

FRANCE

(Country telephone code 33) French Tourist Office, 178 Piccadilly, London W1V 0AL. Tel (24 hour premium rates): 0891 244123. Fax: 0171 493 6594.

Ales, north of Marseilles. Les Compagnons de la Passion, Lycée Technique de la Salle, 2 rue Florian, F-30100 Ales, France. Tel: 0466525421.

Amiens, Somme. 5 times each October. L'Alliance Sainte Anne, 59bis rue Vulfran-Warmé, F-80000 Amiens, France. Tel: Claire Potier 0322912946, Fax: 0322913450.

Gap, Hautes Alpes, south-east of Grenoble. Every Good Friday. Rideau Bleu, 4 Impasse des Rosiers, F-05000 Gap, France. Tel: 0492517640.

Loudeac, Brittany. 2.30 p.m. last four Fri. in Lent. Passion à Loudeac, 11 rue Beaumanoir, F-22600 Loudeac, France. Reservations Tel: 029628 8315. Enquiries: 1521. Fax: 3718.

Maseveaux, south of Strasbourg. La Passion de Maseveaux, Cercle Catholique St-Martin, F-68290 Masevaux, France. Tel: Antoine Weiss 0389824266.

Menilmontant, Paris. La Passion à Menilmontant, 15 rue du Retrait, F-75020 Paris, France. Tel: 146369767. Fax: 147977475.

Mouzon, west of Limoges. Piere Hivert, Services Culturelles, Ville de Mouzon, Mouzon, France.

Nancy, Meurthe-et-Moselle (Lorraine). Théatre de la Passion, 128 Avenue Général Leclerc, F-54000 Nancy, France. Tel: Isabelle Ancemant 0383280880. Fax: 0383359010.

Sainte-Pazanne, 30 km. south-west of Nantes. Feb. to Apr., Sun. 2-6.45 p.m. Enquiries: M. Claude Gireaudeau, 19 rue de l'Ilette. Tel: 0240027389. Bookings: La Pazennaise Théatre locations, 8 rue Beau-Soleil, F-44680 Sainte-Pazanne, France. Tel: 0240027027. Fax: 0240024431.

Salvagnac, between Lyons and Toulouse. Association Foyer d'Amitié, Salvagnac, F-82160 Caylus la Capelle Livron, France. Tel: 0563670861.

Toulon, Mediterranean port south-east of Marseilles. In the 4 weeks before Easter, 1 performance in Toulon & 2 in other towns. Association 'Joyeuse Union de Don Bosco', 455 Bd Jules Michelet, BP 1414, F-83056 Toulon, France. Tel: 0494310847 (Wed. 3-6 pm).

Tullins, French Alps, on the A49, 25 km. from Grenoble. In the 3 weeks before Easter, 8 performances at various times. AEP Passion, Maison Paroissiale, 1 Place de l'Eglise, F-38210 Tullins (Grenoble), France. Tel: 0476078418.

GERMANY

(Country telephone code 49) German National Tourist Office, 65 Curzon Street, London W1Y 8NE, England. Tel: 0171 493 0080. Fax: 495 6129. See under 'German National Tourist Office', page vi.

Auersmacher, south-west of Frankfurt. Junge Buhne, Auersmacher, Josef Lang, Vorsitzender, Sitterswalde Straße 52-54, D-66271 Auersmacher, Germany. Tel: 06805 7589. Fax: 200843.

Bubach. Theaterverein Bubach e.V., Schriftführer Jörg Federspiel, Ringstrasse 27, D-66571 Bubach, Germany.

Hallenberg, north-east of Bonn. Freilichtbuhne Hallenberg, Albert Winter, Urberg 6, D-59969 Hallenberg, Germany.

Kemnath, Landkreis Tirschenreuth, Bavaria. Every 5 years. Last 1998. 5 evenings in the last 2 weeks of Lent, 7.30 p.m. Stadt Kemnath, Stadtplatz 38, D-95478, Bayern, Germany. Tel: 09642 7070. Fax: 707540.

Oberammergau, near Garmisch-Partenkirchen. Last 1990; next 2000. May to Sep., every day except Tue. & Thur., 9-11.30 a.m. & 2.30-5.30 p.m. Verkehrs- und Reisebüro Gemeinde Oberammergau, Ammergauerhaus, Eugen-Papst-Straße 9a, D-82487 Oberammergau, Germany. Tel: 08822 92310. Fax: 7325.

Ötigheim, near Heidelberg. Last 1990; next 2000, Jun. to Aug., Sun., 2 p.m. Volkschauspiele Ötigheim, Kirchstraße 5, D-76470 Ötigheim, Germany. Tel: 07222 22031. Fax: 25272. Internet: http://www.stadtinfo.com/volkschauspiele.ötigheim

Rieden, South of Bonn. Laienspielgruppe des Kath. Junggesellen Vereins, Joachim Engel, Vorsitzender, Oberstraße 66, D-56745 Rieden, Germany. Tel: 02655 1824.

Salmünster, on the A66 East of Frankfurt. Passionspiele Salmünster, Armin Leistenschneider, Fichtenstraße 2, D- 63628 Bad Soden-Salmunster, Germany. Tel: 06056-5654 or 900358. Fax: 2324 or 900356. E-mail A.Leistenschneider@gsi.de

Scheinfeld. between Nurenberg & Wurzburg, Bavaria. Last 1998; next 2002. 6 performances in Jul. Passionspielgemeinschaft

Scheinfeld, K-H & E Guhr, Klosterdorf 33, D-91443 Scheinfeld, Germany. Tel & Fax: 09162 920886. Internet: www.scheinfeld.de
Sömmersdorf, east of Frankfurt. Every 5 years; last 1998; next 2003. Jun. to Aug., some Saturdays and Sundays. Frankische Passionspiele, Robert Seeman, Euerbacher Straße 5, D-97502 Sömmersdorf, Germany. Enquiries: Tel: 09726 3868. Fax: 3660. Tickets: Tel: 2626. Fax: 909066. E-mail Hrueth@t-online.de Internet: http://www.swin.baynet.de/lksw/passion/
Tirschenreuth, north Bavaria. Every 3 years; last 1997; next 2000; Mar. & Apr. 8 performances. Enquiries: Stadt Tirschenreuth, Maximilian Platz 35, D-95643 Tirschenreuth, Germany. Tickets: Postfach 1220, D-95634 Tirschenreuth, Germany. Tel: 09631 6090. Fax: 60949.
Vilgertshofen, near Landsberg am Lech, Bavaria. Sun. after the Assumption. 'Die stumme Prozession', EOS-Druckerei St. Ottilien, Kloster St. Ottilien, D-86941 St. Ottilien, Germany.
Waal, near Landsberg, west of Munich. Passionspielgemeinschaft-Waal, Herrn Assner, D-86875 Waal, Germany.
Wallersheim. Every 5 years; last 1997; next 2002. Fri.–Sun. Klaus-Peter Pauls, Hauptstraße 1, D- 54597 Wallersheim, Germany. Tel: 06558 1093.

HOLLAND
(Country telephone code 31) Dutch Tourist Board, PO Box 523, London SW1, England. Tel (24 hour premium charges): 0891 717777.
Tegelen, south of Venlo. Every 5 years; last 1995; next 2000; Sun., May–Sept. Stichting Passiespelen Tegelen, Postbus 3027, NL-5930 AA Tegelen, Holland, Fax: 077 738628.

HUNGARY
(Country telephone code 36) Hungarian National Tourist Board, 46 Eaton Place, London SW1, England. Tel (24 hour, premium charges): 0891 171200.
Budaors, near Budapest. Bakk Endre Kanonok Alapitvany, a Budaorsi Kulturalis Ertekek, Megmenteseert, Baross U.112, H-2040 Budaors, Hungary. Tel & Fax: 023422 494.
Pécs, South West Hungary.

ITALY
(Country telephone code 39) Italian Tourist Office, 1 Princes Street, London W1R 8AY, England. Tel: 0171 408 1254 or (24 hour, premium charges) 0891 600280. Fax: 0171 493 6695. E-mail enitlond@globalnet.co.uk
Barile, on the Gulf of Taranto. Good Friday 2-6.30 p.m. Comitato Sacra Rappresentazione, Via Roma 29, I-85022 Barile (Potenza), Italy, Tel & Fax: 0972 770062.

Ciconicco, near Venice. Associazzione Culturale Un Grup di Amis, 'Vivens', Via N Pellis 32, I-33030 Ciconicco di Fagagna (Udine), Italy, Tel: Flavio Sialino 0432 801098 Fax: 810568. 7 p.m. Good Fri & Easter Eve.

Grassina, near Florence. Since the 17th century, Good Friday & Holy Saturday, 9.30-11.15 p.m. Enquiries: Centro di Attività Turistica, Rievocazione Storica del Venerdi Santo, 209 Via Chiantigiana, I-50015 Grassina (Firenze), Italy. Tel: 055 642511. Fax: 642011. Tickets on the day of the performance: Via Chiantigiana 226, Grassina.
Internet: http://firenze.net/events/trails/grassina.htm

Pove del Grappa, near Venice. Every 5 years. Last 1995; next 2000. Two weeks in Sep. Comitato Feste Quinquennali, 3 Via Marconi, I-36020 Pove del Grappa, Italy. Tel & Fax: 0424 80327.

Rionero, Potenza. Holy Saturday. Venerabile Confraternita 'Maria SS. Del Monte Carmelo', Chiesadi S. Antonio Abate, I-85028 Rionero in V (Pz), Italy. Tel: 0972 720547. Fax: 0972 721224.

Romagnano Sesia. Every 2 years. Last 1997; next 1999. 3 performances in Passion week. Comitato pro Venerdi Santo, Corso Marconi 17, I-28078 Romagnano Sesia, Italy. Tel: 0163 834742. Fax: 458276.

Sezze, south-east of Rome. Associazione della Passione di Christo, Elio Magagnoli, Via San Carlo, I-04018 Sezze (Latina), Italy. Tel: 0773 886869.Fax: Dr Pietro Formicuccia 803809

Sordevolo, west of Milan. Passione de Sordevolo, Presso Palazzo del Commune, I-13050 Sordevolo, Italy. Tel: Laura Ronchetta 015 2562494. Fax: 2562492.

POLAND
(Country telephone code 48)
Kalwaria, south-west of Krakow. Klasztor oo Bernardynow, ul Bernardynska 46, PL-34-130 Kalwaria Zebrzydowska, Poland. Tel: 33 766-304. Fax: 766-641.

Lobzenica. Misjonarze Swietej Rodziny, Gorka Klasztorna, PL-89310 Lobzenica, Poland.

ROMANIA
(Country telephone code 40) Romanian National Tourist Office, 83a Marylebone High Street, London W1, England. Tel: 0171 224 3692.

Csiksomlyo, a suburb of Miercurea-ciuc, in Transylvania. Every Palm Sunday & Pentecost. Adèle Svella, Hunyadi Jànos 31/A/34, RO-4100 Miercurea-ciuc, Romania. Tel & Fax: 066171770. E-mail cskovacs@csoft.ro

Oradea, near the Hungarian border. Bischof Josef Templi, Str. Stadion Lui 7, Oradea, Romania.

SPAIN
(Country telephone code 34) Spanish Tourist Office, 57 St James's Street, London W1, England. Tel: 0171 499 0901 or (24 hour, premium charges) 0891 669920.

Altea, south of Valencia. La Passio d'Altea, Calle la Mar 24, E-03597 Altea (Alicante), Spain. Tel: 096 5840719. Fax: 5842133.

Cervera, west of Barcelona. Every year for the last 300 years. 10 a.m. - 12.30 p.m. & 3-5 pm. In Castilian language: 5 Sundays in Lent & 2nd Sunday after Easter. In Catalan: Palm Sunday & Good Friday 3-8 p.m., Sunday after Easter at usual times. Enquiries: Patronato de la Passión de Cervera, Av. Paseo Balinas 2-4, E-25200 Cervera, Spain. Tickets: Sra. Mª Theresa Bescós, Pl. Sta Anna 1, E-25200 Cervera, Spain. Tel: 073.530357. Fax: 532946. Internet: http://www.interbook.net/colectivo/passio

Esparreguera, west of Barcelona. In the Catalan Language. Every year since the 16th century. Every Sun. in Mar. and Apr. and the first Sun. in May; 10.15 a.m. - 12.30 p.m. and 3.15 - 6 p.m. Patronat de la Passió, Av. Francesc Marimon 83-89, E-08292 Esparreguera, Spain. Tel: 093.7771587. Fax: 7775519. Internet: www.lapassio.es

Olesa de Montserrat, 37 km. north of Barcelona. In Catalan since 1540. Sundays in Lent, Good Friday and the three Sundays after Easter, 10.15 a.m. - 2.15 p.m. La Passio d'Olesa, c/ Anselm Clavé 109, E-08640 Olesa de Montserrat, Spain. Tel: 093 7781009 Fax: 7785181. E- mail: lapassio@infodisc.es Internet: www.infodisc.es/lapassio

Ulldecona, near Tarragon. Patronato de la Passio, Aparto de Correos 16, E-433250 Ulldecona (Tarragona), Spain. Tel: Isabel Sorli 077 720117. Fax: 573100.

Verges, eastern Pyrenees. Patronat Processo Dijous Sant, Verges (Girona), Spain.

SRI LANKA
(Country telephone code 94)
COLOMBO. A 400 year-old tradition, contact the Portuguese Mission.

SWITZERLAND
(Country telephone code 41) Switzerland Tourism, Swiss Centre, Swiss Court, London W1V 8EE, England. Tel: 0171 734 1921. Fax: 437 4577.

Mendrisio, south of Lugano. Maundy Thursday and Good Friday, procession through the town at 9 p.m. Processioni Storiche Giovedi e Venerdi Santo, Ente Turistico di Mendrisio, Via Angelo Maspoli 15, CH-6850, Mendrisio, Switzerland. Tel: 091 6465761. Fax: 6463348. E-mail etm@tinet.ch

UNITED STATES OF AMERICA
(Country telephone code 1) US Tourist Board, Grosvenor Square, London W1, England. Tel (24 hour premium charges): 0891 600530. The Institute of Outdoor Drama, The University of North Carolina, Campus Box #3240, Chapel Hill, NC 27599-3240, USA. Tel: (919) 962 1328.
Internet: http://www.unc.edu/depts/outdoor/
Arkansas, in the Ozark Mountains. Last Fri. of Apr. to last Sat. of Oct. 1998, daily except Mon. and Thu. Last Fri. of Apr. to the last Sat. of Oct. 1999, daily except Sun. and Wed. The Great Passion Play™, PO Box 471, Eureka Springs AR 72632-0471, USA. Tel: (501) 253 8559 or (501) 253 9200. Fax: (501) 253 2302 or (501) 232 8261. Internet: http://www.passion.org
E-mail: drama@passion.org
Florida. Florida Tourist Board. Tel: (904) 488 5607. Fax: (904) 224 9589.
Florida Tourist Office in London. Tel: 0171 630 6602. Fax: 7703.
St Augustine, Florida. At Easter for a month; Wed. to Sun. 8 p.m.; some Sundays 2 p.m.; Easter Sunday 5.15 a.m. (sunrise). St John's County Passion Play, Inc., P.O. Box 1965, St Augustine, Florida 32085, USA. Tel: (904) 471 1965. Fax: (904) 794 7975.
Lake Wales, Florida. Mar. and Apr. for 6 weeks; Sun., Tue., Fri. & Sat. at 7 p.m.; Wed. and Easter Sunday at 3 p.m. The Black Hills Passion Play, Lake Wales Amphitheatre, POB 71, Lake Wales, FL, USA. Tel: (941) 676 1495. Fax: 638 2037. Freephone in USA 1-800 622 8383. Internet and E-mails as South Dakota below.
Louisiana, Ruston on the US167S. Sep. & Oct., Fri. & Sat. The Louisiana Passion Play, North Louisiana Creative Arts, Inc., 3010 S. Vienna, Ruston, LA 71270, USA. Tel: (318) 255 6277. Freephone in the USA 1-800 204 2101.
New York. Palmyra, Western New York State, near Niagara Falls. Hill Cumorah Pageant. Admission free. 2nd Fri. in July to 3rd Sat. in July, daily except Sun. & Mon. Enquiries: PO Box 403, Palmyra, NY14522, USA. Tel: (315) 597 6808.
North Carolina. Jun. to Aug., Thu. to Sat. 8.30 p.m.; Aug. to Sep., Fri. to Sat. 8 p.m. Worthy is the Lamb, Crystal Coast Amphitheatre, PO Box 1004, Swansboro, NC 28584, USA. Freephone in USA 1-800 662 5960 or Tel & Fax: (919) 393 8373. Internet: www.emeraldisle.net
Ohio. Jun. to Aug., Thu. to Sat. at 7.15 p.m.; Sep. Sat. at 6.15 p.m. The Living Word, 6010 College Hill Road, P.O. Box 1481, Cambridge, OH 43725, USA. Tel: (614) 439 2761. Fax: (740) 439 2761. E-mail livingword5@juno.com
Oklahoma. Jun.to Aug., Fri. and Sat. The Man who Ran, Picture in Scripture Amphitheatre, P.O. Box 190, Disney, OK 74340, USA. Tel: (918) 435 8207. Fax: 8208.
E-mail jonah@brightok.net

South Dakota. Spearfish, in the Black Hills. Jun. to Aug., Sun.,
Tue. and Thu. 8 p.m. The Black Hills Passion Play, POB 489,
Spearfish, SD 57783-0489, USA. Tel: (605) 642 2646. Fax: 7993.
Freephone in USA 1-800 457 0160.
Internet: http://www.blackhills.com/~bhpp/
E-mail: bhpp@blackhills.com
Texas. Jun.to Oct., Fri. & Sat. 8.30 p.m. The Promise, Promise
Productions Inc., P.O. Box 927, Glen Rose, TX 76043, USA,
Freephone in the USA 1-800 687 2661 or Tel: (254) 897 4341.
Fax: 3388. E-mail: Promise@ITexas.net
Internet: www.thepromise.org
Washington State. Jul. and Aug., Fri. & Sat. Jesus of Nazareth,
The Amphitheatre, 14422 Meridian Ave. E., Puyallup, WA 98373,
USA. Tel: (206) 848 3411.

Other Media

As long ago as 1898 Thomas Edison produced a silent movie titled
The Passion Play of Oberammergau. The film *'Jesus of Montreal'* is
required viewing for anyone who wants to think about what effect
it could have on someone to act the part of Jesus. See the reference
book *Jesus at the Movies* by W. Barnes Tatum, Polebridge Press,
Santa Rosa, Cal. USA. See also the novel *Christ Recrucified* by
Nikos Kazantzakis, and Martinu's opera *The Greek Passion* which
is based upon it.

Prayer

Christ our victim, whose beauty was disfigured and whose
body was torn upon the cross; open wide your arms to embrace
our tortured world, that we may not turn away our eyes, but
abandon ourselves to your mercy. Amen

All Desires Known

Prayer

To God be glory; to the angels honour; to Satan confusion; to
the cross reverence; to the Church exaltation; to the departed
quickening; to the penitent acceptance; to the sick and infirm
recovery and healing; and to the four quarters of the world
great peace and tranquillity; and on us who are weak and sinful
may the compassion and mercies of our God come and
overshadow us. Amen.

Syriac prayer

Your Passion Play Hymn Book

These hymns are for singing in church, on the coach, wherever two or three meet together, or individually. They are arranged with their first lines in alphabetical order.

1. All creatures of our God and King,
lift up your voice and with us sing
alleluia, alleluia!
Thou burning sun with golden beam,
thou silver moon with softer gleam,

O praise him, O praise him,
Alleluia, alleluia, alleluia!

Thou rushing wind that art so strong,
ye clouds that sail in heaven along,
O praise him, alleluia!
Thou rising morn, in praise rejoice,
ye lights of evening, find a voice;

Thou flowing water, pure and clear,
make music for thy Lord to hear,
alleluia, alleluia!
Thou fire so masterful and bright,
that givest man both warmth and light,

Dear mother earth, who day by day
unfoldest blessings on our way,
O praise him, alleluia!
The flowers and fruits that in thee grow,
Let them his glory also show;

And all ye men of tender heart,
forgiving others, take your part,
O sing ye alleluia!
Ye who long pain and sorrow bear,
praise God and on him cast your care;

And thou, most kind and gentle death,
waiting to hush our latest breath,
O praise him, alleluia!
Thou leadest home the child of God,
and Christ our Lord the way hath trod;

Let all things their Creator bless,
and worship him in humbleness;
O praise him, alleluia!
Praise, praise the Father, praise the Son,
and praise the Spirit, three in One;

W. H. Draper
(based on St Francis)

2. *All glory, laud, and honour*
to thee, redeemer, king,
to whom the lips of children
made sweet hosannas ring.

Thou art the king of Israel,
thou David's royal son,
who in the Lord's name comest,
the king and blessed one.

The company of angels
are praising thee on high,
and mortal men and all things ∪
created make reply.

The people of the Hebrews
with palms before thee went:
our praise and prayer and anthems
before thee we present.

To thee before thy passion
they sang their hymns of praise:
to thee now high exalted
our melody we raise.

Thou didst accept their praises:
accept the prayers we bring,
who in all good delightest,
thou good and gracious king.

St Theodulph of Orleans
(trans. J. M. Neale)

3. Alleluia! Sing to Jesus!
His the sceptre, his the throne;
alleluia! His the triumph,
his the victory alone:
hark! The songs of peaceful Sion
thunder like a mighty flood;
Jesus out of every nation
hath redeemed us by his blood.

Alleluia! Not as orphans
are we left in sorrow now;
alleluia! He is near us,
faith believes, nor questions how:
though the cloud from sight received him,
when the forty days were o'er,
shall our hearts forget his promise,
'I am with you evermore'?

Alleluia! Bread of angels,
thou on earth our food, our stay;
alleluia! Here the sinful
flee to thee from day to day:
intercessor, friend of sinners,
earth's redeemer, plead for me,
where the songs of all the sinless
sweep across the crystal sea.

Alleluia! King eternal,
thee the Lord of Lords we own;
alleluia! Born of Mary,
earth thy footstool, heaven thy throne:
thou within the veil hast entered,
robed in flesh, our great high priest;
thou on earth both priest and victim
in the Eucharistic feast.

W. Chatterton Dix

4. A Man there lived in Galilee
unlike all men before,
for he alone from first to last
our flesh unsullied wore;
a perfect life of perfect deeds
once to the world was shown,
that all mankind might mark his steps
and in them plant their own.

A Man there died on Calvary
above all others brave;
his fellow-men he saved and blessed,
himself he scorned to save.
No thought can gauge the weight of woe
on him, the sinless, laid;
we only know that with his blood
our ransom price was paid.

A Man there reigns in glory now,
divine, yet human still;
that human which is all divine
death sought in vain to kill.
All power is his; supreme he rules ∪
the realms of time and space;
yet still our human cares and needs
find in his heart a place.

S. C. Lowry (altered)

5. Amazing grace! how sweet the sound
that saved a wretch like me;
I once was lost, but now am found;
was blind, but now I see.

'Twas grace that taught my heart to fear,
and grace my fears relieved;
how precious did that grace appear
the hour I first believed!

Through many dangers, toils and snares
I have already come;
'tis grace that brought me safe thus far
and grace will lead me home.

The Lord has promised good to me,
his word my hope secures;
he will my shield and portion be
as long as life endures.

Yes, when this heart and flesh shall fail
and mortal life shall cease,
I shall possess within the veil
a life of joy and peace.

When we've been there a thousand years,
bright shining as the sun,
we've no less days to sing God's praise
than when we first begun.

John Newton

6. Dear Lord and Father of mankind,
forgive our foolish ways!
Reclothe us in our rightful mind,
in purer lives thy service find,
in deeper reverence praise.

In simple trust like theirs who heard,
beside the Syrian sea,
the gracious calling of the Lord,
let us, like them, without a word
rise up and follow thee.

O Sabbath rest by Galilee!
O calm of hills above,
where Jesus knelt to share with thee
the silence of eternity,
interpreted by love!

Drop thy still dews of quietness,
till all our strivings cease;
take from our souls the strain and stress,
and let our ordered lives confess
the beauty of thy peace.

Breathe through the heats of our desires
thy coolness and thy balm;
let sense be dumb, let flesh retire;
speak through the earthquake wind and fire,
O still small voice of calm.

J. G. Whittier

7. From heaven you came, helpless babe,
entered our world, your glory veiled;
not to be served but to serve,
and give your life that we might live.

This is our God, the Servant King,
he calls us now to follow him,
to bring our lives as a daily offering
of worship to the Servant King.

There in the garden of tears,
my heavy load he chose to bear;
his heart with sorrow was torn,
'Yet not my will but yours,' he said.

Come see his hands and his feet,
the scars that speak of sacrifice;
hands that flung stars into space
to cruel nails surrendered.

So let us learn how to serve,
and in our lives enthrone him;
each other's needs to prefer,
for it is Christ we're serving.

Graham Kendrick
(© 1983 Kingsway's Thankyou Music)

8. Give me joy in my heart, keep me praising,
give me joy in my heart, I pray;
give me joy in my heart, keep me praising,
keep me praising till the break of day.

Sing hosanna, sing hosanna,
sing hosanna to the King of kings!
Sing hosanna, sing hosanna,
sing hosanna to the King!

Give me peace in my heart, keep me loving,
give me peace in my heart, I pray;
give me peace in my heart, keep me loving,
keep me loving till the break of day.

Give me love in my heart, keep me serving,
give me love in my heart, I pray;
give me love in my heart, keep me serving,
keep me serving till the break of day.

Traditional

9. In the cross of Christ I glory,
towering o'er the wrecks of time,
all the light of sacred story
gathers round its head sublime.

When the woes of life o'ertake me,
hopes deceive and fears annoy,
never shall the cross forsake me:
Lo! It glows with peace and joy.

When the sun of bliss is beaming ‿
light and love upon my way:
from the cross the radiance streaming
adds more lustre to the day.

Bane and blessing, pain and pleasure,
by the cross are sanctified:
Peace is there that knows no measure,
joys that through all time abide.

(Repeat the first verse.)

John Bowring

10. Jesus Christ is risen today, Alleluia!
Our triumphant holy day, Alleluia!
Who did once, upon the cross, Alleluia!
Suffer to redeem our loss. Alleluia!

Hymns of praise then let us sing, Alleluia!
Unto Christ, our heavenly king, Alleluia!
Who endured the cross and grave, Alleluia!
Sinners to redeem and save. Alleluia!

But the pains that he endured, Alleluia!
Our salvation have procured; Alleluia!
Now above the sky he's king, Alleluia!
Where the angels ever sing. Alleluia!

Based on *Lyra Davidica*

11. Let us break bread together, we are one.
Let us break bread together, we are one.
We are one as we stand with our face to the risen Son,
oh, Lord, have mercy on us.

Let us drink wine together, we are one.
Let us drink wine together, we are one.
We are one as we stand with our face to the risen Son,
oh, Lord, have mercy on us.

Let us praise God together, we are one.
Let us praise God together, we are one.
We are one as we stand with our face to the risen Son,
oh, Lord, have mercy on us.

Unknown

12. Meekness and majesty,
manhood and deity, in perfect harmony,
the man who is God.
Lord of eternity dwells in humanity,
kneels in humility and washes our feet.

O what a mystery, meekness and majesty.
Bow down and worship
for this is your God, this is your God.

Father's pure radiance, perfect in innocence,
yet learns obedience to death on a cross.
Suffering to give us life,
conquering through sacrifice,
and as they crucify prays: 'Father forgive.'

O what a mystery, meekness and majesty.
Bow down and worship
for this is your God, this is your God.

Wisdom unsearchable, God the invisible,
love indestructible in frailty appears.
Lord of infinity, stooping so tenderly,
lifts our humanity to the heights of his throne.

O what a mystery, meekness and majesty.
Bow down and worship
for this is your God. This is your God.
This is your God.

Graham Kendrick
(© 1986 Kingsway's Thankyou Music)

13. Morning glory, starlit sky,
leaves in springtime, swallows' flight,
autumn gales, tremendous seas,
sounds and scents of summer night;

soaring music, tow'ring words,
art's perfection, scholar's truth,
joy supreme of human love,
memory's treasure, grace of youth;

open, Lord, are these, thy gifts,
gifts of love to mind and sense;
hidden is love's agony,
love's endeavour, love's expense.

Love that gives, gives ever more,
gives with zeal, with eager hands,
spares not, keeps not, all outpours,
ventures all, its all expends.

Drained is love in making full,
bound in setting others free,
poor in making many rich,
weak in giving power to be.

Therefore he who thee reveals
hangs, O Father, on that tree
helpless; and the nails and thorns
tell of what thy love must be.

Thou art God: no monarch thou,
throned in easy state to reign;
thou art God, whose arms of love
aching, spent, the world sustain.

W. H. Vanstone (© J. W. Shore)

14. My song is love unknown,
my saviour's love to me,
love to the loveless shown,
that they might lovely be.
O, who am I that for my sake
my Lord should take frail flesh, and die?

He came from his blest throne,
salvation to bestow
but men made strange, and none ∪
the longed-for Christ would know.
But O, my friend, my friend indeed,
who at my need his life did spend.

Sometimes they strew his way,
and his sweet praises sing;
resounding all the day
hosannas to their king.
Then 'Crucify!' is all their breath,
and for his death they thirst and cry.

Why, what hath my Lord done?
What makes this rage and spite?
He made the lame to run,
he gave the blind their sight.
Sweet injuries! Yet they at these ∪
themselves displease, and 'gainst him rise.

They rise, and needs will have ∪
my dear Lord made away;
a murderer they save,
the prince of life they slay.
Yet cheerful he to suffering goes,
that he his foes from thence might free.

In life no house, no home,
my Lord on earth might have;
in death no friendly tomb,
but what a stranger gave.
What may I say? Heav'n was his home;
but mine the tomb wherein he lay.

Here might I stay and sing,
no story so divine;
never was love, dear king,
never was grief like thine!
This is my friend, in whose sweet praise
I all my days could gladly spend.

Samuel Crossman

15. Now thank we all our God,
with heart and hands and voices,
who wondrous things hath done,
in whom his world rejoices;
who from our mother's arms
hath blessed us on our way
with countless gifts of love,
and still is ours today.

O may this bounteous God
through all our life be near us,
with ever joyful hearts
and blessed peace to cheer us;
and keep us in his grace,
and guide us when perplexed,
and free us from all ills
in this world and the next.

All praise and thanks to God
the Father now be given,
the Son, and him who reigns
with them in highest heaven,
the one eternal God,
whom earth and heaven adore,
for thus it was, is now,
and shall be evermore.

> M. Rinkart
> (trans. Catherine Winkworth)

16. O sacred head, surrounded
by crown of piercing thorn!
O bleeding head, so wounded,
so shamed and put to scorn!
Death's pallid hue comes o'er thee,
the glow of life decays;
yet angel-hosts adore thee,
and tremble as they gaze.

Thy comeliness and vigour
is withered up and gone,
and in thy wasted figure
I see death drawing on.
O agony and dying!
O love to sinners free!
Jesu, all grace supplying,
turn thou thy face on me.

In this thy bitter passion,
good shepherd, think of me
with thy most sweet compassion,
unworthy though I be:
beneath thy cross abiding
for ever would I rest,
in thy dear love confiding,
and with thy presence blest.

P. Gerhardt
(trans. H. W. Baker)

17. **On a hill far away stood an old rugged cross,**
the emblem of suffering and shame;
and I love that old cross where the dearest and best
for a world of lost sinners was slain.

So I'll cherish the old rugged cross
till my trophies at last I lay down;
I will cling to the old rugged cross
and exchange it some day for a crown.

O, the old rugged cross, so despised by the world,
has a wondrous attraction for me;
for the dear Lamb of God left his glory above
to bear it to dark Calvary.

In the old rugged cross, stained with blood so divine,
a wondrous beauty I see;
for 'twas on that old cross Jesus suffered and died
to pardon and sanctify me.

To the old rugged cross I will ever be true,
its shame and reproach gladly bear;
then he'll call me some day to my home far away,
when his glory for ever I'll share.

George Bennard

18. **Praise to the holiest in the height,**
and in the depth be praise:
in all his words most wonderful,
most sure in all his ways.

O loving wisdom of our God!
When all was sin and shame,
a second Adam to the fight
and to the rescue came.

O wisest love! That flesh and blood,
which did in Adam fail,
should strive afresh against the foe,
should strive and should prevail;

And that a higher gift than grace
should flesh and blood refine,
God's presence and his very self,
and essence all-divine.

O generous love! That he, who smote ⌣
in man for man the foe,
the double agony in man
for man should undergo;

and in the garden secretly,
and on the cross on high,
should teach his brethren, and inspire ⌣
to suffer and to die.

(Repeat the first verse.)

J. H. Newman

19. Ride on! Ride on in majesty!

Hark! All the tribes hosanna cry!
O Saviour meek, pursue thy road
with palms and scattered garments strowed.

Ride on! Ride on in majesty!
In lowly pomp ride on to die:
O Christ, thy triumphs now begin
o'er captive death and conquered sin.

Ride on! Ride on in majesty!
The wingèd squadrons of the sky
look down with sad and wondering eyes
to see the approaching sacrifice.

Ride on! Ride on in majesty!
The last and fiercest strife is nigh:
the Father on his sapphire throne
awaits his own anointed Son.

Ride on! Ride on in majesty!
In lowly pomp ride on to die;
bow thy meek head to mortal pain,
then take, O God, thy power, and reign.

H. H. Milman

20. Spirit of the living God,
fall afresh on me;
Spirit of the living God, fall afresh on me.
Break me, melt me, mould me, fill me.
Spirit of the living God, fall afresh on me.

Daniel Iverson
(© 1935, 1963 Moody Bible Institute)

21. *Thank you, Jesus, thank you, Jesus,*
thank you, Lord, for loving me.
Thank you, Jesus, thank you, Jesus,
thank you, Lord, for loving me.

You went to Calvary, and there you died for me,
thank you, Lord, for loving me.
You went to Calvary, and there you died for me,
thank you, Lord, for loving me.

You rose up from the grave, to me new life you gave,
thank you, Lord, for loving me.
You rose up from the grave, to me new life you gave,
thank you, Lord, for loving me.

Unknown

22. The Lord's my shepherd, I'll not want;
he makes me down to lie ∪
in pastures green; he leadeth me ∪
the quiet waters by.

My soul he doth restore again,
and me to walk doth make ∪
within the paths of righteousness,
e'en for his own name's sake.

Yea, though I walk through death's dark vale,
yet will I fear none ill;
for thou art with me, and thy rod ∪
and staff me comfort still.

My table thou hast furnishèd
in presence of my foes;
my head thou dost with oil anoint,
and my cup overflows.

Goodness and mercy all my life
shall surely follow me;
and in God's house for evermore
my dwelling-place shall be.

Unknown

23. There is a green hill far away,
without a city wall,
where the dear Lord was crucified,
who died to save us all.

We may not know, we cannot tell,
what pains he had to bear,
but we believe it was for us
he hung and suffered there.

He died that we might be forgiven,
he died to make us good,
that we might go at last to heaven,
saved by his precious blood.

There was no other good enough
to pay the price of sin;
he only could unlock the gate ∪
of heaven, and let us in.

O dearly, dearly has he loved,
and we must love him too,
and trust in his redeeming blood,
and try his works to do.

                    Mrs C. F. Alexander

24. Thine be the glory, risen, conquering Son,
endless is the victory thou o'er death hast won;
angels in bright raiment rolled the stone away,
kept the folded grave-clothes where thy body lay.

Thine be the glory, risen, conquering Son,
endless is the victory thou o'er death hast won.

Lo! Jesus meets us risen from the tomb;
lovingly he greets us, scatters fear and gloom;
let the church with gladness hymns of triumph sing,
for her lord now liveth, death hath lost its sting.

No more we doubt thee, glorious prince of life;
life is nought without thee: aid us in our strife;
make us more than conquerors through thy deathless love;
bring us safe through Jordan to thy home above.

                    E. L. Budry
                    (trans. R. Birch Hoyle)

25. To God be the glory! great things he hath done!
So loved he the world that he gave us his Son,
who yielded his life an atonement for sin,
and opened the life-gate that all may go in.

Praise the Lord! Praise the Lord!
Let the earth hear his voice!
Praise the Lord! Praise the Lord!
Let the people rejoice!
O come to the Father through Jesus the Son;
and give him the glory, great things he hath done!

O perfect redemption, the purchase of blood!
To every believer the promise of God;
the vilest offender who truly believes,
that moment from Jesus a pardon receives.

Great things he hath taught us, great things he hath done,
and great our rejoicing through Jesus the Son:
but purer and higher and greater will be
our wonder, our worship, when Jesus we see!

Frances van Alstyne
(Fanny J. Crosby)

26. Were you there when they crucified my Lord?
Were you there when they crucified my Lord?
Oh, sometimes it causes me to tremble, tremble, tremble;
were you there when they crucified my Lord?

Were you there when they nailed him to the tree?
Were you there when they nailed him to the tree?
Oh, sometimes it causes me to tremble, tremble, tremble;
were you there when they nailed him to the tree?

Were you there when they laid him in the tomb?
Were you there when they laid him in the tomb?
Oh, sometimes it causes me to tremble, tremble, tremble;
were you there when they laid him in the tomb?

American folk hymn

27. When I survey the wondrous cross,
on which the prince of glory died,
my richest gain I count but loss,
and pour contempt on all my pride.

Forbid it, Lord, that I should boast
save in the death of Christ my God;
all the vain things that charm me most,
I sacrifice them to his blood.

See from his head, his hands, his feet,
sorrow and love flow mingling down;
did e'er such love and sorrow meet,
or thorns compose so rich a crown?

Were the whole realm of nature mine,
that were a present far too small;
love so amazing, so divine,
demands my soul, my life, my all.

Isaac Watts

Blessing

Christ crucified draw you to himself, to find in him a sure
ground for faith, a firm support for hope, and the assurance of
sins forgiven; and the blessing of God almighty, the Father, the
Son and the Holy Spirit, be among you and remain with you
always. Amen.

The Alternative Service Book 1980

An artist's impression of the hill of Calvary.

Learn a Phrase a Day

There are many fluent English speakers among the people of Germany, Austria and Switzerland. However, it is a sign of friendliness to make some attempt to learn the German language. Without over-taxing the memory, it is quite possible to learn a few simple phrases each day during a holiday in these countries. Here are some suggestions. Ask a German speaker to demonstrate the pronunciation.

Each of the sections below follows this format:
1. English phrases.
2. German translations.
3. German pronunciation.

1. Good morning. Good evening. Good day.
2. Guten Morgen. Guten Abend. Guten Tag.
3. Gootun morgun. Gootun aabunt. Gootun taak.

Bavarian dialect forms:
1. Hello. Goodbye.
2. Grüss Gott. Pfüat di Gott *(intimate)*. Pfüat eich Gott *(plural or formal)*.
3. Grüs got. Pfüert dee got *(intimate)*. Pfüert eye-ch got *(plural or formal)* *('ch' as in 'loch'; the 'ü' (u umlaut) is half-way between 'ee' and 'oo')*.

1. Where are the toilets? Men. Ladies.
2. Wo sind die Toiletten? Herren *or* Männer. Damen *or* Frauen.
3. Voh zint dee toy-lettun? Hairun *or* mennur. Darmun *or* frowun *('ow' as in 'shower')*.

1. See you again. *(On the telephone:)* Hear you again.
2. Auf Wiedersehen *or* Auf Wiederschauen. Auf Wiederhören.
3. Owf veedurzayun *or* Owf veedershowun. Owf veedurhörun *('ö' is almost the same vowel as in 'dirt', 'curds' etc.)*.

1. How much does that cost? One, two, three, four, five, six, seven, eight, nine, ten Euros.
2. Wieviel kostet das? Einen, zwei, drei, vier, fünf, sechs, sieben, acht, neun, zehn Euro.
3. Veefeel kostut dass? Eye-nun, tsv-eye, dr-eye, feer, fünf, zeks, zeebun, archt *('ch' as in 'loch')*, noyn, tsayn Oy-roe.

1. It costs eleven, twelve, thirteen, twenty, twenty-one, thirty, a hundred and one German Marks. No, it is too dear.
2. Es kostet elf, zwölf, dreizehn, zwanzig, ein und zwanzig, dreissig, einhunderteine Deutsche Mark. Nein, es ist zu teuer.
3. Ess kostut elf, tsvölf, dr-eye-tsayn, tsvantsich, eye-n oont tsvantsich, dr-eye-sich, eye-n hoondurt eye-nuh doytchuh mark. N-eye-n, ess ist tsoo toyur.

1. We would like two beers/ three coffees with milk, please. No, no sugar, thank you.
2. Wir möchten zwei Bier/ drei Kaffee mit Milch, bitte. Nein, keinen Zucker, danke.
3. Veer möchtun tsv-eye beer/dr-eye kaffay mitt milch, bittuh. N-eye-n, k-eye-nun zookur, dankuh *('ch' as in 'loch')*.

1. What time is it? One o'clock, five past two, a quarter past three.
2. Wieviel Uhr ist es? Ein Uhr, fünf Minuten nach zwei, Viertel nach drei.
3. Veefeel oor isst ess? Eye-n oor, fünf minootun naach tsv-eye, feertul naach dr-eye.

1. Half past four; a quarter to six; early tomorrow; too late.
2. Halb fünf; Viertel vor sechs; Morgen früh; zu spät.
3. Halp fünf *(literally 'half five')*; feertul for zeks; morgun frü; tsoo shpät *('ä' as in 'spare')*.

1. Where is there some hot water? Cold water? Iced water? Thank you very much! It's a pleasure!
2. Wo gibt es heisses Wasser? Kaltes Wasser? Danke schön! Bitte schön!
3. Voh Gibt ess h-eye-sus vassur? Kaltus vassur? Dankuh shön! Bittuh shön!

1. What is the weather like today? It is raining. The sun is shining. It's going to snow.
2. Wie ist das Wetter heute? Es regnet. Die Sonne scheint. Es wird schneien.
3. Vee isst dass vettur hoytur? Ess raygnut. Dee zonnuh sh-eye-nt. Ess veert shn-eye-un.

1. We need a double room with bathroom or shower.
2. Wir brauchen ein Doppelzimmer mit Bad oder Dusche.
3. Veer browchun eye-n doppultsimmur mitt baat owe-dur dooshuh.

1. Breakfast. Lunch. Dinner. A snack. Something to drink.
2. Frühstuck. Mittagessen. Abendessen. Imbiss. Etwas zu trinken.
3. Früshtük. Mitaagessun. Aabuntessun. Imbiss. Etvass tsoo trinkun.

1. Help! Danger. Forbidden. Police. Fire. Doctor. Dentist.
2. Hilfe! Gefahr. Verboten. Polizei. Feuer. Arzt. Zahnarzt.
3. Hilfuh! Guhfaar. Fair-boat-un. Pollits-eye. Foy-uh. Artst. Tsaanartst.

1. Give me medicine for my wife/ my husband. Stomach ache. Headache.
2. Geben sie mir Medizin für meine Frau/ meinen Mann. Magenschmerzen. Kopfweh.
3. Gaybun zee meer maydeetseen für m-eye-nuh frow *('ow' as in 'now')*/ m-eye-nun mann. Maagunshmairtsun. Kopfvay.

List of Illustrations

Colour photographs by the author

© 1998 Michael Counsell

On the cover:
Neuschwanstein
A ceiling at Ettal Abbey
A model of the set for the opening tableau of the Oberammergau
   Passion Play in 2000

Colour photographs by Thomas Klinger

*Pictures of the Oberammergau Passion Play in 1990, used by kind
permission of the Village Committee.*

114

Drawings by Chan Borey

Pictures of Passion Play scenes from earlier years. (Chan Borey is a Cambodian artist working for Southeast Asian Outreach in Phnom Penh.)

Index of Scriptures, Sources and Acknowledgements

SCRIPTURE PASSAGES

SOURCES AND ACKNOWLEDGEMENTS

Alexander, Mrs C. F. (1818–95) 108

All Desires Known, © Janet Morley (expanded edition, SPCK, 1995), used with permission from SPCK 94

Allon, Henry (1818–92) 6

American folk hymn 109

Anselm, St (1033–1109) 12

The Alternative Service Book 1980 (*ASB*) (© Central Board of Finance of the Church of England), reproduced by permission 6, 9, 110

Baker, Sir H. W. (1821–77) 105

Bennard, George 105

Bowring, John (1792–1872) 100

Brent, Charles Henry (1862–1929, Bishop of the Philippines, then of Western New York), in *With God in Prayer* (George W. P. Jacobs & Co., 1907) 68

British Library (reproduced by permission of the British Library, Ref. 1390) 6

Budry, Edmond (1854–1932) (public domain) 108

The Church of South India, attributed to *The Book of Common Worship of the Church of South India 1963* (original source untraced; reprinted by permission of Oxford University Press) 23

Compline, adapted from the *Sarum Breviary* by Edward Willis in the *Cuddesdon Office Book*, 1880 85

Counsell, Michael, in *More Prayers for Sundays* (HarperCollins*Liturgical*, 1997, © Michael Counsell) 38, 58, 59

Crossman, Samuel (1624–83) 103

Dix, W. Chatterton (1837–98) 97

Dostoevsky, Feodor (1821–81) 35

Draper, W. H. (1855–1933) (© J. Curwen & Sons Ltd, 8–9 Frith Street, London; reproduced by permission) 96

St Francis of Assisi (1182–1226) 96

Gelasian Sacramentary (fifth century) 3, 46

Gerhardt, P. (1607–76) 105

Horae BVM (pre-fourteenth century) 75

Hoyle, R. Birch (1872–1939) (public domain) 108

Huntingdon, William Reed (1838–1909) 42

Iverson, Daniel (© 1963 Birdwing Music/ EMI Christian Music Publishing; administered by Copycare, PO Box 77, Hailsham, BN27 3EF, UK; used by permission) 107

Kendrick, Graham (© 1983 & 1986 Kingsway's Thankyou Music, PO Box 85, Eastbourne, East Sussex, BN23 6NW, UK; used by permission) 100, 102

Liturgy of St John Chrysostom 65

Lowry, S. C. (1855–1932) (copyright owner unknown) 98

Lyra Davidica (1708) and others 101

Milman, H. H. (1799–1868) 106

Neale, John Mason (1818–66) 96

Adapted from *A New Zealand Prayer Book – He Karakia Mihinare o Aotearoa 1989* (with permission of the General Secretary, the General Synod Office, Hastings, New Zealand; of the Church in Aotearoa, New Zealand and Polynesia) 58

Newman, Cardinal John Henry (1801–90) 106

Newton, John (1725–1807) 98

The Prayer Book as Proposed in 1928 (© Central Board of Finance of the Church of England; reproduced by permission) 79

St Richard of Chichester (1197–1253) 82

Rinkart, M. (1586–1649) 104

Roman Missal (Excerpts from the English translation of the *Roman Missal* © 1973, International Committee on English in the Liturgy, Inc. All rights reserved.) 27, 54

'Saviour of the World', from a Congregational Hymnal 1862 edited by Henry Allon (1818–92); see *The Alternative Service Book*

Scottish BCP (*The Book of Common Prayer 1929*), by permission of the General Synod of the Scottish Episcopal Church 15

Index of Subjects

Your Notes

Your Notes